FROM THE FORMAL LOUNGE ROOM

In Conversation with My Grandfather

The life of Cav. Felice Zadro told
in his own words

Interviewed and written by
Felicity Zadro

Copyright © 2025 (Felicity Zadro)
All rights reserved worldwide.

No part of the book may be copied or changed in any format, sold, or used in a way other than what is outlined in this book, under any circumstances, without the prior written permission of the publisher.

Inspiring Publishers
P.O. Box 159, Calwell, ACT Australia 2905
Email: publishaspg@gmail.com
http://www.inspiringpublishers.com

 A catalogue record for this book is available from the National Library of Australia

National Library of Australia The Prepublication Data Service

Author: Felicity Zadro
Title: From the Formal Lounge Room:
         In Conversation with my Grandfather
Genre: Non-fiction, Memoir

Paperback ISBN: 978-1-923250-70-3
ePub2 ISBN: 978-1-923250-71-0

Dedication

To Nanna, for the millions of ways you showed your enduring love; the cups of tea, the thousands of handmade gnocchi, for always being excited to see us, the way your heart grew every time a new one was born, your unwavering and innate optimism, your faith in each of us, the heart-to-hearts, the laughs, the hugs, and kisses. Thank you for it all.

To Catherine, only the memory of THOSE hugs can dull the pain of your passing.

To my darling Georgina, little did I know it would take your tiny perfect hands to inspire mine to pick up the pen again.

Only by being true to oneself,
can one act from a position of strength.

—Hannah Arendt

*One generation shall commend your works to another,
and shall declare your mighty acts.*

—Psalm 145:4

CONTENTS

Author's Note ix
1. Leaving Home 1
2. Working in Australia 24
3. Making Smithfield Home 56
4. Building Community and a New Home 80
5. Inspiring a Legacy 115
6. Raising a Family 131
7. Faith and Politics 161
8. Life 186
Photos 202
Articles 214
Acknowledgements 245
About the Author 248

AUTHOR'S NOTE

I understood he felt he was nearing his time when my grandfather, *Cavaliere* (Cav.) Felice Zadro who we called *Nonno*, asked me to help him collect his memories and write a biography of his life. Although he was often out of breath due to his emphysema, at the time we sat down and had these conversations he was eighty-six years old and as sharp as a tack; in fact, he was this way until his last day of life. It was a remarkable thing; however, he often felt his body and mind were not seemingly of the same age.

Two months before he died, he threw a 60th wedding anniversary dinner for his wife, our Nanna. A week before he died on 8 August 2006, a senior leader of his beloved Club Marconi, a large social and sporting club in Bossley Park, New South Wales (NSW), Australia, that he helped to establish, visited him to seek his counsel. I walked into Nanna and Nonno's house and there he was, breathing machine and all, listening and providing guidance. A couple of days before he passed, the kettle blew. He went out into the shed, pulled apart an old kettle that had been sitting there for more than 25 years, removed the element, wired it into the broken one, and fixed it. Then Nanna made the tea. That was Nonno. He was ninety-four when he died.

It has been a long time between putting down the pen and picking it back up again on this project. I loved the experience and the time we spent together, me with my pages and pages of prepared questions broken into chapters, I felt represented the themes of his life and Nonno, with his mind ready to reminisce. We went together to the local shopping centre and bought a tape recorder that we could use to record these sessions and arranged times and dates when we could talk. It was decided that the mornings were better for Nonno, and so Nanna would tuck us away in the formal lounge room, door closed, with tea and biscuits, as we'd embark on our conversations.

We traversed his life through his eyes, with me as his willing bystander. I would prod him to be more emotional and reveal inner thoughts while his preference was to stick to facts.

I wanted to understand what he felt, what his fears were and what it was to wear the badge of a non-English speaking new migrant. What it did to his staunch pride to be called derogatory names when people didn't understand him or where he came from, or what he had to contribute, or who he really was.

At times, Nonno was reluctant to go there, so we went where he allowed. This is his story.

I tried to keep him on track most times, but one memory would spark another; and he enjoyed where his mind took him. So, we talked about a bushranger in the middle of telling the tale of courting Rina, my grandmother, and we talked of Italy in the same breath as Smithfield, where he made a home in NSW—often losing himself in the memories of his youth.

Whilst the initial transcriptions have been edited to ensure the following pages are easy to read, I've been careful to retain his voice, and his turn of phrase, so to capture what it was like to talk with him.

My hope is that for those who knew him, that after reading this, you'll feel like I do … that you've just finished your cuppa with him at the round table in their home at Bossley Park, with the blind half down; the SBS news just about to start, and the birds chirping in the background.

The stories Nonno told me in our times together stuck like glue to my heart. I couldn't shake them from my daily thoughts. They ultimately became a powerful influence that has shaped my view of the world and of him, and of all migrants and families who have moved countries for economic, political, or personal reasons. Knowing, so intimately, his life stories have inspired me in many ways.

In fact, ten months after he died, I founded my own business and named it after him. His dedication to community and connection becoming the core mission of the organisation, touching many who have never even heard of him.

Whilst Nonno's stories in this book, were told by him, they are not only of him. For no one does it alone. Is it the stones that shape the river, or the river that shapes the stones? This is how we must interpret the stories—especially considering Nonno's mother, Maria Zadro nee Morassut, and his father, Giuseppe Zadro, whose responses to the way their lives were shaped by WW1, are the reason why Nonno came to Australia—which was fundamental to whom he became. And thirdly, Rina Zadro nee Spinelli, his wife of sixty years, whose love and faith enabled Nonno to do so much out of the home, whilst keeping the home-fires burning. This partnership of two people's lives so firmly intertwined was the fuel for the fire that inspired and enabled so much. Nanna is inseparable from what is often heralded as Nonno's achievements: *his* story, is so definitely *her* story, in this case.

There are so many great anecdotes within these pages. Look out for the *cocodrillo* tale; the horsemanship; the pride he felt when Nanna was thrilled to be pregnant; the desperation to get their Smithfield farm back, after it was unlawfully taken from them during WWII; his disgust at the soldier who accompanied him to see his first-born son in hospital whilst being interned, who left to go to the pub; his dogged determination to be released from internment; the start of Club Marconi and his presidency, and the honour he felt at being named *Cavaliere* by the Italian Government.

I don't claim that the words written here are final, or even all the truth. Every one of our large family — especially his four children — will have their own versions of the events that are mentioned here. They might even feel that half-truths or even rose-coloured glasses have been applied. I don't know. I wasn't there, but I can only assume. These are his words.

My hope is that this is a memory-jogger for all who knew him, or those who share a similar story of migration and family, so that you can remember in your own way, your own time, and your own memories of the years, the struggles, the love, and the determination.

I still miss Nonno. I miss our heated arguments about politics and society. But mostly, I miss his frankness and the way he would just cut straight to the point.

"What are your intentions with my granddaughter?" He'd ask just four questions into meeting a new boyfriend. "Tell me what is happening in your life," he'd say. And when I, and no doubt others, were a little sheepish, he would say, "If you can't tell me, then you aren't proud of what you are doing; and if you aren't proud of what you are doing, you shouldn't be doing it." Words to live by.

So why pick up the pen now? I feel like I'm sitting on family treasure and not sharing it with my extended tribe. I want my daughter to know a bit of the man who helped shaped me. I want to honour my Nanna with it, and finally, as our family grows and changes, as we lose people and we get busy with our own, I want to ensure the glue that binds us is as steadfast as Nonno would always have wanted it.

Postscript

Our dear Nanna, Rina, died on 23 October 2019 after an eight-week bout of illness. She knew I had started this project again, as I desperately took in this section, the Author's Note, when I had the chance, and asked her if I could read it to her, as she was bedridden in Liverpool Hospital, New South Wales (NSW). She remembered the times I interviewed Nonno and she thanked me for sharing it with her.

It was the last coherent conversation I had with my Nanna.

CHAPTER ONE

Leaving Home

"I pinched three or four potatoes; gave them the potatoes, and they gave me the cigarettes."

Would you like to start Nonno? Do you want to start talking about where you are from?

My name is Felice Zadro. I was born on 13 April 1913 to Maria (Morassut) and Guiseppe Zadro. My place of birth is *Sesto al Reghena* (north-east Italy). It is an old town that goes back more than a thousand years. Before describing its history, I should proceed with my younger days in this historical town.

I was born in 1913, and my youth was through the First World War, when my father and his four brothers were at war. When the German-Austrian army invaded our town, we were deprived of everything that we had: food of any description, livestock, even linen.

Did the soldiers take those things from you?

Yes. Everybody was at war, all the men were at war, we were only there with an uncle who was crippled, my grandmother who was a widow, my mother, and the three children (that my dad had). Of course, we had to house the Germans who were in our area, and this lasted for quite a long time. They lodged in our home; they took part of our rooms; they were living in our house. They used to go and come and come and go, all the time. Unfortunately, they were very hungry, as their rations were very, very poor (because now I am talking about 1918). When the Germans left our premises, they told us they were going to the *Fiume Piave,* and that is when the war was ending. A sergeant—a gentleman soldier—left me a piano accordion, and he kept telling us, "*Piave ... kaputt.*" That means, "We are going to die at this river." It is very sad remembering this; I was only a young child, but I vividly remember.

At this time, my dad and my three uncles were at the front fighting. We lost one uncle, Louie, to the war. Finally, the war ended, and Dad and his brothers came back home.

You can just imagine; we were deprived of everything. When my father left, at the beginning, we had a couple of beautiful horses, and we also had chickens and ducks. Everything went. They (the Germans) deprived us of everything because they were very hungry, too.

I remember two soldiers asking for something to eat and they made the shape of potatoes. They must have known that my grandmother had some potatoes, and they told me where she kept them too. So, they showed me that if I gave them some potatoes, they would give me some cigarettes, so I did. I pinched three or four potatoes, gave them the potatoes, and they gave me the cigarettes. I was five years old, because this was 1918. Then I went behind the house, and I started to smoke the cigarette, and I got violently sick. My family were all wondering what had happened to me. Finally, when they discovered what I had done, I was punished. Anyway, this is one of the encounters that I remember. There are other trivialities that I can recall: the soldiers marching, regiments and canons, guns placed differently around the place and all of this business. Soldiers marching with the rifles, and as I was young, I would march with them because I was impressed by the left-right, left-right, and them talking in their own language.

I remember that there was a curfew (no one was to go out) because the Austrian Emperor was passing through; but me, being young and cheeky, I went out onto the road and watched the parade. This was early 1918, just before the end of the war. Franz Joseph[1] came to inspect his army, and I went out and stood there on my own, watching the parade go past.

The Austrian Emperor was coming to inspect his troops. In the parade, there were horses and cavalry, everyone was mounted, and the carriage was something very elaborate. There were soldiers on top at the back and the drivers for the horses. The carriages were driven by four or six horses, and the front horses were mounted.

What a contrast, to have something so elaborate go through the area that had just been totally devastated by the war.

Yes, no one was to go out because they were concerned for their safety due to the Austrian Emperor.

Anyway, then when Dad came home, we had grown up a bit, and he narrated to us children about his episodes at war. He was decorated for having shot down a German plane. Because of this, he had earned holidays, but of course he could not come home, at that time, because the Germans invaded our area; we had Germans all around us.

So, then the war ended, and we were very short of meat. There was no meat about and one day, when the men were

---

[1] Franz Joseph I (1830-1916) was Emperor of Austria along with his wife, Empress Elizabeth of Austria, Queen of Hungary. He was King of Hungary and many other states in the Austria-Hungarian Empire.

out on the farms, they saw something climbing up a cherry tree. They had a shotgun with them all the time because they were hoping that they would find something to cook up and make a stew. Anyway, my uncle shot it, and they took the skin off it, and took it home to my nanna. It was a rabbit, and she cooked it up and everyone was around feasting on this rabbit.

I said genuinely, "Uncle was very smart, shooting that rabbit on top of the cherry tree." Everyone looked at each other ... we were eating a cat! Everyone got up, left the table, and went outside.

How long was your father away from your family?

Well, from 1915-1918, four years had passed. Dad was four years in the trenches, and he contracted cholera and he nearly died with it and things of that nature. Anyway, my dad and two uncles finally came home, they organised the farm again, and the government supplied machinery to do the ploughing until they were able to get together a bit of stock that was imported from other nations, Switzerland mainly.

They used to plough with the bullocks and cows; they would pull the single plough and that was the industrialised world of those days. Cows, a single plough, bullocks, and horses doing all of the work. It happened that the owner of the land that my parents were on, working on half-shares, started to sell the property.

This happened in 1923. So, my father and his brothers decided to buy a plot of land and to build a house on it.

My father, at that time, had five children, you see. Of course, he had to find a place to accommodate them, and so together with another brother, Emilio, (and another uncle), they decided to build three houses on this block of land. They acquired a bit of land to grow something, and they built the houses one next to the other, along the road, along *via Mura* from *Sesto*.

Sadly, they found out that it wasn't enough to sustain the family; there was no work because of the Depression that set in after the war. So, they decided to leave for Australia. An opportunity arose for my uncle to go to Australia. He left his wife with a child. My uncle worked at the Steel Works, in Lithgow, NSW, and he got my father to join him because he knew my father was even worse off than he was because of his bigger family.

My father joined him in Australia, although there was a depression in Australia too, and it was very hard to get a job. My father finished up unable to work with my uncle in the Steelworks and he got transferred from there to Port Kembla, NSW. But, when they were transferred, the workers from Lithgow were dismissed. During this time, my father got some work at an ironworks, and then from there, he finished off in Merriwa at Brindley Park, with a gang of migrants cutting Bathurst burrs.

Bathurst burrs is a weed that grows very profusely, with little berries on it with thorns. These berries stick to the wool of sheep and there was no way of getting them out because they were like hooks.

Then from there, he decided to go and seek work at another station. He finished up going to a station called Warringalah. The owner of Warringalah was Wardell. Wardell's father was the premier of NSW in the absence of the then premier.

I'd like to stop you there and go back a bit more for information about Italy. You are the eldest of the family, aren't you? How many brothers did you have?

Yes, I am the eldest. There were five brothers; we lost one when he was a baby — it was a boy. My parents had three of us: me, Davino, and Louie. Then my father went to war and when he came back, they had Luciano (aka Chana) and Tarcisio (aka Terry).

What was it like being the eldest?

Well, being the eldest, I became responsible, more or less, for the wellbeing and the care of my aunty, my grandmother, my uncle (who was a bit of a cripple), and myself. So, I had to do the running about for all of them. I was trusted to do things left and right, and I was only a child.

But even before that, when your father was at war?

Well, no, I was only a child. I never had any responsibilities. I only had the gift of giving potatoes away for cigarettes (he laughs).

Were you close to your brothers when you were younger?

Oh, we were close enough, but Louie (the third brother), he was a little bit of a demon, and he didn't like school. He used to wag school and go bird nesting with another three of his mates. Of course, we had trouble keeping him at school and I had to chase after him and look for him and chastise him in a certain manner because he was the youngest of the three. I was responsible for getting the crops home and collecting them and getting the fields worked. I used to go to the cousins, and they used to come and plough the land for us and put the seeds in; and, of course, I had to look after the crops.

Not much time for school then?

Before this happened, the owner of the land, he was *Count Tullio* and there were three or four brothers. One was in parliament in Italy, and another was a professor in medicine. They were very well-to-do people, of course. They used to live in a town 8-9 kilometres from where we were, called *San Vito al Tagliamento*.

Oh, the things that went on there is something unbelievable. My father rented ten acres of land, rich in soil. He hired a tractor to plough and a driver, because someone had to hold the plough. There were only single ploughs in those days, and he put in a crop of corn and then left for Australia. I was entrusted with looking after this crop. When the harvesting time came along, I had to get my cousins, the *Morassuts* (my cousins on my mother's side) to come and help us gather all the corn. We had to store the corn somewhere, so we rented a loft in a building which was four flights of stairs up and we had to get all the corn up to the top. I remember that I was trying to compete with the men; I was carrying these bags of corn up the top. Oh!

So many things like that happened, that it is not funny. This was part of the life in those days. I was going to school, but before I went to school, they used to get me up at 4.00 am to drive the cows and the bullocks on the plough, you see, because they were set in two. And we had to drive them along and turn them around and then, of course, when school time came, they sent me to school. I was too tired when I got to school; I wanted to sleep. Never mind ...

In the summertime, we went to school, but in the winter, there were three months of recess. It was too cold. Like I was saying before, my father built these houses in 1924. The houses still exist. After the war they had been modified, but they were two storeys with a terrace, stables for the cows, and barns for the pigs. All of these things were provided for and that's how we used to live. We had chickens, we had ducks, we used to keep geese, they all needed to be fed; we used to give them grass here and there.

That was life in those days, and we were quite happy, but now that I am telling you these things it makes me wonder how we ever did it. In spite of the poverty, we were still as happy as you could be; we used to joke, laugh, and we used to play.

Do you think the happiness was something that your mum and dad felt as well or was it just that you were a child, and you did not understand the situation?

No, Dad was very worried, I must confess. He was very worried because he could not see a future in the situation that he was in. He was out contracting because he had a licence for driving and he was driving this tractor with a machine for the wheat. And he used to go from one place to another, from one house to another, because we were all agricultural people and we used to all grow wheat, and they had to thrash it.

Dad used to go with the tractor and the machine. He used to go to other places and set it up with another man who helped him with the thrashing and everything. He did that for about a month at the most, because the area was restricted, and it wasn't a very big district.

Anyway, everyone used to look after their own district. We could not go and do this next door, because there was someone else there. So anyway, from there, he used to trust us to look after the cows, the pigs, and the chickens, and we used to go to the farm and gather grass and things for the animals.

Mum, the poor soul, never had running water. But what happened is my aunty got her brothers to dig a well. One of her brothers came over and picked the site for the well. The brother turned around and told us what to do. I was digging, and we had this round cylinder, these round concrete pipes about 4-feet in diameter. You had to pass it down and you dig, and you dig, and it goes down and then you put another one on top and you keep going and going. We finished up having five of these. They were a meter-and-a-half tall — five of these on top of the other — until we got to the water. I was there filling the buckets up and this brother of my aunty used to wind it up and take the water. I soon was right down at the bottom of the well, me and my cousin, Sante.[2] He passed away some time ago.

So, we got the water, the drinking water, which we had never had before. Before this, my mother used to go and get the water from her brother's place about 200 metres away. She used to have a stick across the shoulders with two buckets on each side. Finally, when we got the water in this well, we put a pump on it, and we used to pump and fill these buckets and take them home.

How old were you when you started to go to school?

When I started, it could have been about 1920 (seven years old). Well, then I had experiences there too.

Did you like school?

I had to like it. I had to learn. I didn't mind it, it was primary school, and it was very intensive study. When you finished

---
[2] Father of Maria and Margaret Zadro

fifth class, you knew about geometry, and you knew about history and geography. The learning was very intensive and very good too.

I was in fifth class, just beginning the scholarly year, and we had a teacher who was crippled; he had a wooden leg. He used to get a girl to open up the school around 8.00 am or 8.30 am but he never came to impart any lessons until about 10.30 am or 11.00 am. You can just imagine what was going on in that class. We were mixed with boys and girls; there could have been about 25-30, maybe more … thirty-five.

One day, I got fed up with this. I incited everyone to walk out and go home and we were about to go home, and he came in. He walked in mid-morning, and he said, "What is going on here?" This red-headed girl went and told him that I was responsible; I was organising the strike to walk out.

Oh, he belted me. He gave me a hiding. He kicked me and I had black eyes. My cousin Sante, who was also involved, and I got expelled from school. I was only in Year 5. I was twelve. Anyway, Dad decided to get private tuition for me, and we used to go into town to these teachers for lessons.

So, you went home and told your dad about being expelled?

Dad saw me with my black eyes, but they couldn't do anything about it. Because in that time, fascism was taking place, it was the beginning of it. The party was not organised or settled, but it was beginning and there was a lot of movement against it and for it. And this schoolteacher was a fanatic fascist.

What did that mean to you being twelve years old when someone said, "Oh, he is a fascist?"

Nothing; politics never affected me, but the fascist government really organised the schools. You'd be surprised by the difference it made. Fascism as it was, was very abrupt to impose themselves, but the benefits that Italy got out of it, in the beginning, were fantastic. But the damage they have done at war was atrocious.

But anyway, this teacher forbade me from going to school and then he forbade these private teachers to give me lessons!

How did he have that power?

Because he was the headmaster, and being the headmaster, that is what he could do. One day, my father was in town, and he was getting gravel to build our houses, this was in 1924, in the very beginning. He was with his wagon and the horses, carting this gravel to make some cement, and he was going through the town, and he met up with this teacher. This teacher was already drunk because he used to go and play cards and drink. Anyway, my father excused himself and said, "*Signore Maestro*, why don't you allow my son to go to school? After all, he is only a kid?" The teacher got my father by the chest, because to him my father was a peasant. Talking to the headmaster the way he did was unheard of. He grabbed my father as if to say, *How dare you!* He had one of those mentalities.

My father said, "You let go or I'll crack your head with the whip; I'll strip your brains with it!" So, the *maestro* put his hands in his pockets and, of course, Dad suspected he had a gun. Dad said, "You take your hand out of your pocket, or I'll bust your brains." So, he did take his hands out of his pockets. The *maestro* then turned around and people had gathered around to see what was happening. He said, "One, two, three, four; you will be a witness that Zadro attacked me!"

"Oh yes, we will be witness ... that you attacked Zadro!" They said.

But I didn't go to school.

So, what did you do with your days, then?

I used to get books and study ... I would like to think back a bit and try and do a little reminiscing on my religious imparting. We used to get catechism. We used to go before school for an hour from 8.00 am until 9.00 am. It was imparted by a chaplain, and the parish priest, and some nuns. Of course, they were preparing us for Holy Communion, and we had to learn the prayer in Italian, as well as in Latin. They would give us a sort of exam to see whether we learnt enough and then they accepted us for Holy Communion.

Then it came time for Communion. Holy Communion was a feast in the family and then Confirmation was a bigger feast because we had a sponsor for confirmation, and they usually gave you presents. The present that you received was a watch or money or something like that. I had a watch that I treasured for many, many years.

So, you got a watch, did you? Who did you get that off?

Off my sponsor, his name was Vit Emilio, but he is long dead now. He was a family friend. That family was under the same mayor that I told you before, the one that my parents were under, the landowners. The imparting of the watch was very appreciated.

There were gatherings of youths, and we had a youth centre: The Catholic Youth Centre. We used to have outings and all of this. Then fascism came along, and every town had a *Balilla (8-15-year-olds fascist movement)* but, in our town, there was nothing like that. We had a terrific mayor, and although he was fascist himself, he never imposed anything. He was working with the church and there were no bashings or anything in town, you know. They accepted the fascism. There were critics, but they were talking amongst themselves.

I remember in one instance there were quite a few of the town's people together, gathering in our place. They were talking about fascism and what could they do to get through their point of view. And I remember as a kid I said, "Well, the sure way to put your view to the government is to become one yourself."

"Well, listen to him!" They said.

Anyway, they told me, "Get out you little skimp!" Nothing was done about it, I'm sure.

What was your mother like?

Oh, my mother was holy, she was really fantastic. She used to teach us and Dad too, you know. Dad was a real believer and a real Catholic. There was no two ways about it. There was no swearing. He went to church every Sunday. Even in Australia, here without our mother, he always went to mass; it didn't matter what. He couldn't understand the priest, but he still went to mass. He knew the routine and everything that was going on. Anyway, that comes after, so …

What led up specifically to your father leaving?

Well, the hardship. The poverty. The Depression and having no work.

My father followed his brother in 1927.

It was nothing to do with fascism?

No, nothing to do with politics. Nothing was sordid. In fact, he was very well respected, by the whole family, by the town, by the mayor, by everybody.

I still remember the mayor. He was a very gracious sort of person, a big fellow, you know, and the town used to worship him, in a sense for what he believed and the decorum he kept in every facet of life.

So, when did your father decide to leave?

Well, I don't remember dates. My uncle left in 1925. Two years after, in 1927, my father left for Australia, and he had to borrow money for the trip. He borrowed money to build the houses, buy the land, and was in debt. Then he had to borrow money to come to Australia, and he was lucky that someone did lend him the money. He was writing all the time when he was in Australia. You can just imagine, every week we used to get a letter. Oh yeah.

How long before you received the letters that he wrote?

A month, a month-and-a-half. They used to travel by ship in those days.

Do you remember your father leaving?

Yes, frankly, you know, it was a gloomy day, and the cousins took him to the station, *Portogruaro*, and from there he went to Genoa, where he embarked on a boat that took him to Australia.

What was it like when he left?

We were crying our eyes out. His mother (my grandmother) crying, everybody was crying. Well, yes, everyone was crying. When he got this job that I was telling you, in this Warringalah—Wardell's place—he was writing and telling us what he used to do. He used to ride a horse, and he used to muster cows, and round sheep, and then he finished up by sending photos. And, of course, that got me excited. I got very excited to see all of this ...

So, when your father left, did things get harder for you being the eldest son?

Yes, because of the responsibilities that fell on my shoulders, as I said before, that didn't induce me to leave, you know, I was just excited to travel. Just imagine, I only had caught the train, once before! And that was when I went to see my brother, Davino in college. Everything was new to me, but then when I caught the train from *Portogruaro*, to go to Genoa, ah![3]

Now I am jumping, but anyway, when my father asked me if I would like to go to Australia, I said, "My word I would like to go to Australia."

Did you know anything about Australia then?

No, nothing.

Did you know where it was?

Oh, geography; I had an idea where it was, on the other side of the world. Anyway, we started by getting ready to travel. Of course, I had to get clothes to take with me. Anyway, my father sent photos and wrote, but finally we got all the papers together, the passports ...

---

[3] Portogruaro is a town and commune in the Metropolitan City of Venice, Veneto, in Northern Italy.

Did your mother want you to go?

On no, nobody wanted me to go. I was only fifteen. I had only caught the train once before, and this was the second time. I will tell you a little story about the journey. From *Portogruaro* to Mestre Station, a city where trains exchange as there are different lines, we had to wait for four hours for a train from Milan. It was winter and very cold, and they had one of those portable stoves in the station which had to be kept burning with coal and wood and things. There was an attendant there, I offered to help him. He said, "Alright."

While I was there, another woman came, with a child—a little girl—she was going to Australia, as well. And her brother accompanied her, Romanello their name was. Before meeting this Mrs Romanello, I was getting anxious about which train to catch because there were trains coming and going. I was thinking, *will I miss the train?* The anxiety! *Will I catch the right one?* There were these two fellows, and I asked them. They saw me with this big suitcase, and I said, "Tell me please, is this the train from Milan?"

"Oh yeah, yeah, yeah, you better get on it," they said.

I got suspicious, and I didn't get on it; just as well. So anyway, after that episode, I went back to the waiting room with the fire and this woman comes along with a child. I was there stoking the fire, and this little girl came over close to it and something happened that the door almost fell out from the stove, the one that closes the fire. It was a near miss, and I was very, very concerned and worried. The attendant said, "See what you are doing? What are you doing?"

Anyway, that was all right and everything was fixed up. Then we proceeded finally, to the right train. The woman had a brother who knew all about what to do, so I got on with them and I stayed with them until we got to Milan. In Milan, we had to change trains again. We went from one platform to another. And of course, I had to drag this suitcase. Finally, we got to Genoa, and at Genoa, they had a hostel, and we all stayed in there. In this hostel, they compelled everybody to have baths. Our belongings had to be fumigated before boarding the ship. The ship that we were boarding was a converted commercial liner. Just after the war, there were diseases and fleas, so they had to disinfect everything and make sure that everything went through this heating system.

Anyway, finally I went on board the ship and presented my papers. "Oh," they said, "who is accompanying you?"

I said, "This lady so-and-so." But that lady didn't get on at Genoa, she wasn't there. "Oh," they advised, "we can't allow you to go if you haven't got a sponsor, someone has to be responsible for you." Being too young, you know.

So, they thought fit to ask someone. They asked this fellow if he would be responsible, if he would put his name down to be responsible for me during my journey to Australia. He accepted, and this fellow turned out to be a drunkard and I finished up looking after him!

So, when you got onboard and when you caught the train down to Milan and changed, what were you thinking about?

I was worried; *Am I doing the right thing? Am I catching the right train?* These were my thoughts until I got on to the boat. We went through the narrow Strait of Messina making our way to the Suez Canal. Once we went through there, the boat was going a bit like an earthquake, and I will never forget that this is where I became a bit seasick. I remember going through the Suez Canal and, every now and then, you'd see a group of local boys naked on the shores, exposing their genitals to everyone on the boat. Youngsters, you know.

Were you scared?

On no, I was okay. Finished up, we got out of the Suez Canal at Port Said, Egypt and the boat broke down. We had to stop for quite a few days at Port Said while the boat was getting repaired, and it was stinking hot. That is where I tasted my first banana, and I thought it was awful. The first mouthful I got and the feeling of sweetness of it!

While we were there, they employed all of the local boys to do the cleaning of the boat. The funny thing about that was they used to have a billycan with them, and they used to get their meal with the billycan and when they went to the toilet, they still had the billycan to wash themselves with. After seeing the toilet, I remember remarking on these things because I had become friendly with the other passengers, and we all were wondering what was going on. And we asked the Commissioner of Boats, who was responsible for the behaviour of migrants, of the travellers.

Well, the boat got going again. The journey was long and slow; it took about ... we left Genoa on the 18th of December, and we landed in Sydney on 14th of February. That is not counting the travel from my own town, from Sesto to Genoa. That is just the sea voyage.

What was it like? It must have been horrible!

Oh, the boat was horrible. We never had cabins. We had this big, call it a hall if you like, in the hold of the boat, it was all bunks, one on top of the other.

How many people were on the boat?

Oh, four or five hundred or more, I forget now, because some got on at different ports and some got off.

But the boat was very ... the people were getting annoyed; they didn't know what to do with themselves. They used to play games; we used to play a game like this: We'd all put our arms criss-cross in front of us, and all line up and you had to figure out whose arm belonged to who.

Of course, they used to get into squabbles, and this officer, he didn't like this type of business because we used to finish up with arguments.

"I'll tell you what do to do," he said, "make two lines of all the passengers facing each other, face-to-face and back-to-back." There were some young fellows there, twenty-four or twenty-five, and they added, "Yeah, we will do that, get us some women!"

You must have been so bored. What did you eat on the boat?

Sometimes it was all right, but sometimes it finished up that we all got an attack of gastro, or diarrhoea; it was terrible, the agonising pain and burning. During the journey, the worst part was the sick feeling.

Another experience that I thought was funny was there were three bunks on top of one another. I was on the top bunk and on the next one was this young fellow. He was a very athletic Italian. He was there mending one of his shirts, but he had no shirt on at the time. He had all his chest and top of the body exposed and he had the chest that was really protruding, it looked like the bosoms of a woman. But it was all muscle. Anyway, what happened was this other fellow wanted to organise a kind of sport for the ship. He went down for his inspection of the migrants to see who would be interested, and he saw this fellow sitting on his bunk, and he looked at him and said, "There is a woman down there!" He went and got the captain, and he took them all down there and they all looked and laughed. He didn't know what was happening.

Were there any babies born on the boat?

No.

Do you remember coming into Sydney?

Yes, I remember it. First, what we saw of Australia was Freemantle, Western Australia. Then, we travelled some more, and we had sighted a few homes and then we reached Sydney and there was Dad waiting for me. We stayed with him at this boarding house, and we stayed there for two or three days, and Dad took me around a bit in Sydney. He showed me a few sights of the area, but not very much. This is in 1929.

What was it like to see your father? You hadn't seen him for two and a half years!

Oh, you can just imagine. Dad was jumping up and down. "Is it you? You've grown up. Look at you, you are a man!"

By then I was really developed; I didn't grow any more in height because I worked too bloomin' hard carrying these bloomin' bags of corn up to the tenth floor.

When we finished, he took me to Merriwa, we caught the train, and he took me to the station where he worked.

What did you think of Sydney?

Well, for me, I had no knowledge of cities, except a big town like *Pordenone* or *Portogruaro*. I went to *Vicenza* once, you know that is where Davino was, and I saw the city there, but I was more concerned with finding the place and getting back to the station and doing the right thing, by catching the train. You know, not being used to anything.

And was this the first time that you were in a country that didn't speak Italian?

Of course! When I went to *Vicenza*, I had never caught a train before. We didn't know how to get out and how to get on and that sort of thing. Or where to sit. Have you the right to sit down? These things that are normal now, they used to be problems. You can just imagine.

We went from Merriwa to Warringalah (NSW), to the Wardell's. This was where my Uncle Emilio was.[4] By then, the steelworks at Lithgow had closed up and my uncle was without a job, so Wardell, my father's boss, gave him a job too. He was there for a little while then Wardell found him a job at another station which was Mount Erin and the owner there was Roach; a staunch Catholic. He was decorated by the state.

So, my uncle went to work there, and I stayed with Dad, but he never had work for me, because the place was small. You know what Wardell got me to do while I was there? He got me two kerosene tins; you know the four litre kerosene tins? And he had a ten-acre paddock of lucerne, and it had a lot of stones in it, rocks, and he got me these two tins and I had to go to this paddock, fill the things up with rocks

---

[4] The words, Uncle and Zio, are used interchangeably throughout.

and then throw them over the fence. It was like from here to Cowpasture Road.[5] Those ten acres, ah! I thought, *Is it possible that I came to Australia to do this? To carry this?*

Did you regret your decision?

No, I didn't regret anything. Dad gave me my first lesson of riding a horse and things of that nature. Dad would go out into the paddocks, and I would go out with him on a horse, chasing cows and sheep (of this nature). I felt quite at home.

But one day, I offended my father. One day, he prepared the table for the meal, and he took out butter and jam and cheese. When I saw the butter and the bread I said, "But Dad, Mum used to sell the butter to buy groceries and things for us, and you eat butter, we are eating butter, isn't it enough to eat the bread without the butter?"

Oh, Dad was so, *'ah'*, but that was the truth, you know. We used to milk the cow, make the cheese, make the butter, and then we used to sell the butter. And I was reminding him that he was doing the wrong thing. More or less, I reprimanded him for using butter. On top of that I asked, "Isn't bread good enough?"

It is a stupid thing to remember, but I remember it because I offended my father.

Well, it is interesting, because you had come all this way and you didn't really know what your father had been doing for all this time. I think it shows a little of the impact of the distance and time you had apart.

---

[5] Bossley Park Road down to Cowpasture Road, Bossley Park, NSW roughly 600 metres.

CHAPTER TWO
Working in Australia

"Let the little Italian do it, he is strong."

Back to Australia ...

Well now, I did say that my Uncle Emilio was there with my dad and when I arrived here, he got another job that Wardell got for him. The job was at Mount Erin and the owner of that ranch was Mr Thomas Roach.[6]

There was no work for me at Wardell's, so Dad went to town to see if he could get work for me. There he met a manager, Mr Thompson. He was looking for men for burr cutting. Dad rode to town, ten kilometres or more, and he got talking to this man and he told my dad that he would give me a job. Dad told me that there was a job for me and so Dad called a taxi to come. I had to get everything bundled up, and I was to go to Merriwa in the taxi.

I got into the taxi with this man and, of course, my English was nil. This man was driving and singing to himself all the time. It took about one hour. He took me to a woolshed; it was nighttime. The woolshed comprised a place for where they cut the wool, a place to shear the sheep, and a vast floor where they stored the bale after the wool was pressed into bags. They call them 'wool bales'.

He brought me into this big barn and there I put down my blankets and I slept on the floor. Next morning, of course, no breakfast; I didn't have anything to cook with and I didn't know what to do. Working for this man, Thompson,

---

[6] Mr Thomas Roach was a free settler from Clare, Ireland.

was an Italian man, and he was from *Montebelluna*. This man had his son working for him, as well. His son was a couple of years older than I was, but I never met him. The boss asked him to cater for me, but it wasn't only him, there were another two Italians and one of them was a man I came over with on the ship. Thompson split the other two, and they were to provide for themselves. Me and the older chap, we had our own utensils, and we had to cook for ourselves. We used to get by; I would have a sandwich for breakfast and so on.

We were working there in the woolshed, and I was there for a while. I was chipping burrs in the paddocks after that, we cleared the paddocks around the house. They got a dray with a horse, a tank, and a few utensils, and took the two of us up to another property of Mr Thompson's.

On the way up with this horse and cart, we came across this beautiful garden and two houses. We were travelling along the flat of a creek and the house was up a slope, halfway up a hill. It looked fantastic, and I thought to myself, *My goodness, I wonder if I would be lucky enough to get a job at this place. They must be very nice people, look at the beautiful garden, look at the beautiful ...* this and that. I said a prayer to God that he might help me get a job in there one day.

We went further on, and we put up our tent. The tent was a two-man tent and there were four of us. We didn't have mattresses, so we cut grass and branches, and we made up the floor of the tent to sleep on, one next to the other. Anyway, we put the blankets on top of this rubbish and lay on the blanket.

We had the cooking to do, and this old fellow knew how to do everything. I was the *bocia*, like 'you youngster'.

He would say, "You wish you had your mother here to cook for you, ah, you youngster! Hey, you!" All this was going on all the bloomin' time, on and on and on. We were there for about a month, in this situation, the four of us.

Then it started to rain. The creeks started to flood something terrible. We were getting our rations every Thursday evening from town. The mail man used to have a buggy with two horses, and he used to take the mail and the groceries with things that people had ordered, with deliveries and things like that. He couldn't come across because of the floods, so we finished up having nothing to eat for two weeks. The only thing we had was coffee, black coffee. We used to drink black coffee, and I was shaking. We had three days with nothing to eat, nothing at all.

Finally, we got a bag of bread, you know, the corn bread. The mailman came up with this bag of bread and some mail for the others (not for me). I remember the square loaves that they used to make in those days. I ate one without anything. I got a loaf and just ate it. I didn't have time to sit down.

Were you homesick?

Oh, I certainly remembered Mum very often and while I wasn't feeling too good, I used to get concerned. Dad, he knew that I had a job, but he didn't know where I was. So, what he did was he found out through his boss who the person was that gave me the job. They gave Dad directions of where Thompson was and because he hadn't heard from me for a good three weeks, he got his horse and, with a pair of pliers in his pocket, he took off cross-country to come and see what I was doing and how I was.

This was a Sunday and what happened was we had just had something to eat, a bit of soup with some rice. We boiled some shanks of lamb, and the broth used to smell of bloomin' sheep! Anyway, no sauce, no cheese, nothing you know. So, we put bread in it. The boss used to supply the lamb.

On this Sunday, Zio Emilio—he was halfway between me and Dad at Mr Thomas Roach's—he knew where I was, so he came to see me. It was dinnertime, and we offered him what we had. He ate it and said, "If you haven't got anything better to give me, don't expect me over anymore." (laughter).

He went home and when he got home, the boss, Mr Roach, told him that my dad called, and he was making his way to where I was. So Zio Emilio came back and said, "Has your father been here?" because it was getting dark. I told him, "No."

"Oh, he is lost in the bush," said Zio.

So off he went, looking for him in the area. He found him and together they got home. Dad was as pale as a ghost. He never had anything to eat, and his horse was standing with his legs out in exhaustion. We gave him something to eat there and Zio Emilio said, "You better go and have something to eat at my place."

So, my dad went back to Zio's place and had something decent to eat. Zio used to be a good cook and very fussy, too.

We got shifted from that position into another paddock, but this time we were closer to where Zio Emilio was. And of course, I got to know about it and I decided to pay a visit. I walked over and I remember this: this group of cattle were looking at me, they lifted their heads and I thought, *Oh, no!* I kept walking, and they were coming and coming, and I started to run, and they started to run. Ah! I finished up looking for where the fence was, and I made for the fence. I jumped over the fence and the cattle came up to the fence and stopped there.

Then, I learnt that they chased me because I ran. I shouldn't have. I should have stopped and tried to frighten them off. Of course, I learnt that afterwards.

Did you have any contact with your family in Italy at that stage?

Oh no, only Dad had contact with Mum at that stage. They sent letters to Dad. Oh, they used to communicate every three or four weeks. We used to get a letter one way or the other.

Anyway, I went to see my uncle. We finished that job and my uncle said, "There might be work for you here. Mr Roach is clearing this flat along the creek, to clear it up to grow lucerne on it." There were a lot of trees and stumps and one thing and the other, so it finished up that I got a job there. I went with Zio Emilio. He used to cook and cook very well. I was alright! I'd go out to the bush with the other men sometimes and he'd give me sandwiches.

One day, there was a festival in town and Mr Roach was a very proud Catholic, with all his family. He had three daughters and a son. They used to go to church every Sunday, although they had twenty-four miles to go. The Queen also decorated him; he was a very astute person, knowledgeable and wealthy.

Anyway, one day, we had to pile up all the wool, timber, roots, stumps, and branches, and heap them all up ready to burn. They left the task to me, to light all of this timber. Zio Emilio had to go somewhere else with his horse, on another part of the property. Mr Roach went into town, and they left me the job to burn all of this timber. What I did, I lit the whole lot. And there was ten acres, there was a lot. Mr Roach came home and said, "That nephew of yours, what did he do? When I was approaching the place, I thought I was going to hell with all of the fire that was about!" Anyway, I'd done the wrong thing, I shouldn't have burnt the whole lot because they wanted some wood to heap up again for when the fire went out and so forth. But anyway, I did it.

That job was finished, and he got a ploughman in. He had about eight horses in the team, pulling this plough. So, he had no more work for me.

Another thing I noticed was he had these three daughters and when I used to work around the house, the girls used to peep through the window. I thought to myself, *Wow!* But they were never allowed to come out of there, you see.

Did you ever get to meet them?

No, no. In those days, migrants—Italians—we were a 'low breed'.

So, Mr Roach told Zio, "Look, I haven't got any more work here for your nephew, but I won't send him away until I get him a job." He was a decent man, a very decent fellow.

He did get me a job. One Sunday, a Buick (car) comes on the scene to pick me up. This was Mr Noble. Young Mr Noble. It was getting dark, and I went with him across the country, across creeks, and I am saying to myself, *I think that I have been here before. Is it possible that there is another place that this resembles as much?*

It got dark, very dark. He pulled up to his garage and then he gave me a kerosene lantern and he said, "Come with me." I followed him and he took me down to the shed. This shed was made of slabs with split logs, standing up for walls. The floor was the same, with split logs and it had a fireplace. The fireplace was two big round stones, and the chimney had two sheets of iron put together. There was a stretcher, a wire stretcher. I put my things on it, and I plonked on this stretcher. I didn't have anything to eat or anything, I just plonked there, and I slept!

The next morning, when I woke up, the sun was up. I went out the door and I looked out and I thought, *Goodness me! What did I do?* I had slept in. I rushed up to the house, and there I met the boss, and he didn't say a word. He asked me if I slept well and one thing and the other. There was also another man getting the horses from the yard and saddling them up because they were going out into the paddocks, mustering or doing chores and fencing, and things of that nature.

I was there too, and they gave me a horse and a saddle to put on it. I didn't know which way to put it. I managed to put the bridle on it, and I was wondering how to do it … I had never used one before. They told me to go into a paddock and get all the cows and bring them into the yard.

Did you understand them?

I understood enough. Between cows and horses, I had ridden a horse before with my father; I went out with him for my first time. I went and got the mail. The mailbox was at least 2km away. We had to cross a creek to go to the mailbox and I remember getting to the mailbox. After I rode the horse for the first time, I couldn't walk. But anyway …

I managed to go and get these cows. I was cantering along looking for these cows and all of a sudden, the horse shakes; he nearly threw me off, because he shook on one side. I regained my stirrups and everything and when I looked around, there was a tree, a stump. It was a dead tree, about six-foot-high, and it had a dead branch sticking out and you know what was sticking out? A huge, big lizard. I had never seen one before. I regained my position on the saddle and started yelling, "*Cocodrillo! Cocodrillo!*" I thought it was a crocodile. No more cows! I went home. The men were still about when I was yelling, "*Cocodrillo, Cocodrillo, Cocodrillo!*"

You should have seen them doubling up with laughter. I felt as small as … well, I felt very humiliated. I found out later that it was a bloomin' lizard, and it a big one too.

I had my chores, but I wanted to do everything that the other men were doing. The boss, Mr Noble Snr, lived in Sydney with his wife and daughter. The wife was an asthmatic; that is why they had two houses. The old house was the home of Mr Noble Snr and the new house, the second house, was the son's, with his wife. They had no children and occasionally, Mr Noble Snr used to come up to Merriwa. He used to stay there a week, two or three, and then he would go back. He would be in contact with his wife. If his wife wasn't feeling too well, he would leave and go back to her.

What happened shortly after I arrived was Mr Jack Noble Jnr and his wife used to go and visit his mother in town. They would stay away for three, four, sometimes five weeks. They had another foreman on the other side of the creek from where I was, and they used to have this hut for shearers, and there was a man who had four sons, but his sons were in town and his wife had died. He also had a daughter, and she was married in town. Sometimes, he used to spend time with the youngest of his sons; Sid was his name, and he was a year younger than I was. He used to come over sometimes and I used to give him a meal, because he wasn't working; he wasn't doing anything.

Sid and I decided to take a ride and see if we could climb this hill. We could see it in the distance, and there was a brown patch on the very top. Everything was brown with no trees. They used to call it the 'bluff' because nobody could get up there with a horse. Sid was going to go up and then he decided he didn't want to, so one day, I decided to go myself.

One Sunday, off I went with the horse. I got up as close as I could, but I couldn't go up with the horse anymore, so I walked. I walked up and the brown patch that we could see in the distance were all broken ferns. They were taller than I am, and it was humid up there … the humidity! There was moss everywhere! But all of a sudden, I saw a big hole that like, ooh! *Gee whiz!* I thought, *What the devil could that be?* I was really a bit scared and concerned, you know.

I left the hole, and there was another one; then I went to the top. From up there I looked around, and everything was smaller. I started to sing, and I listened to my echo. I thought that from up there I was closer to Italy, that is how young I was. After I had done that, I had a romantic feeling. I felt really forlorn and alone.

What were you thinking about in particular about Italy?

I was thinking about my mother, my brothers, my friends, and things that I did, you know, the games, the town and all of these things.

(Going back to before)

When I told you that the Nobles used to go into Sydney, I remember a time around Easter. They used to stay away for a month because there was the Sydney Show (the Easter Show), every year. They'd leave me in charge, yet I could hardly speak English. My duties were to kill sheep for food for all of the men when they got back from work. They used to go to Merriwa, you see. They all went to Merriwa to their families, and I was up there on my own. I had my chores to do.

How long were you by yourself?

Two weeks. Usually, the men were given a fortnight's holiday around Easter. I had the chore to go around the cow paddock. This is where I saw this 'crocodile' of mine. I was climbing up this hill with my horse and I was happy. I could see the vastness of everything ... the hills, the green, the blue skies and I thought, *Oh, isn't this beautiful?* I started to sing the songs that I learnt in Italy. I was singing and my horse was climbing up and then all of a sudden, I looked around and I thought, *Gee, I am here on my own. If anything was to happen, what would I do?*

Were you scared?

Oh no, I wasn't scared, but I realised the position I was in. Anyway, finally I said to myself, "I think I'd better say a prayer if anything was to happen to me." And I did pray. I said a Hail Mary and Our Father and things like that. And then I proceeded with my job.

Again, I found myself camped with the cows, and they were all there except one. And the stray one was on top of this hill. I couldn't go with the horses, so I tied the horse up and I went to round up this cow. This bloomin' cow! I got it down from the top, but instead of going with the other cows, she took off down this gully near a slope. It was full of trees, you know. So, I hurried up, got on my horse and went off after her. Going down the hill, the horse had to put pressure on its stomach. And all of a sudden, the belt underneath the horse broke, and I tumbled over. I fell off the horse!

Next thing, I came to. I must have been unconscious for quite a while; I came to, and I muttered, "Gee, what happened?" I looked around, and there was my horse, asleep, waiting for me. Usually, they'd run off, but this horse was so faithful that it stopped there, and my prayers had worked. I found the horse was there, the saddle over there, I was amongst the rocks. I went to get up and oh my ribs! I had a swollen eye; I was in a bloomin' mess. I had scratches everywhere.

I got the horse on the lower part of the hill, and I managed to throw the saddle on its back. And then I walked home. I left the cattle, and I walked home.

I thought, *Gee, what am I to do now?* I went to lie down, but oh my ribs … the pain! My eye, I couldn't see out of one eye. The other one was damaged too. *Ah goodness! What am I to do now, up here on my own?*

After a while I heard the sound of a car! Oh, a car! *It must be one of the men coming back*, I thought. But it was too early. I went outside and I could see this guy coming up. This fellow came up and you know who it was? The fellow that picked me up from Merriwa and gave me the first job.

He was going along the creek, there was a water spring. That road went to the top of the hill I was telling you about before. It was a beautiful flat area. There were exotic trees, and it was green, and he had his girlfriend and that is where he was going for a picnic.

When he came over and saw me, I moaned, "Please, doctor!" He put his hand on me and said, "Oh, my goodness."

He took me to the doctors in Merriwa and on the way to Merriwa, I was sick as a dog. With the pain and the bouncing of the car, I passed out. I was unconscious three or four times. He got me to the doctor, and the doctor got me on his table. He bandaged me with tape. Turned out that I had three broken ribs. He gave me drops to put in my eyes, and then they sent me back!

When I got back, I couldn't lie down, I couldn't sit down, I had to cook for myself. Oh, what a bloomin' struggle! Anyway, I never despaired or anything, I didn't cry or anything. I was managing the best way I could. Then I finished up getting a little bit better as time went on, then the boss came home.

Before this, one of the chores that I had was the killing of the sheep and weighing the meat to give it to the men when they came back. I had to keep a list of it, in my own way; I used to write in Italian. So many pounds of this, so many pounds of meat, what was from the store? Salt, pepper, flour, etc.

When the boss came home, it was in the evening and it was dark, so I went up to welcome him. Because he had a garage where the old house was and the old house from the hut (my house) was a bit of a distance, about 200 metres. I used to go through his garden and a paddock. I'd go up but I couldn't speak very much.

"How is everything?" He asked. "Oh me, doctor," I replied.

Just imagine, Mr Noble had driven all the way from Sydney. He had opened the fourteen gates and crossed the three creeks and now he thought he had to go back to town!

"Oh no, I have already been to the doctors," I said in my own way.

"Oh, thank God for that!" He said.

Well anyway, that was one of the dramas that I had.

Generally, how would you say Italian migrants were treated?

Well, in the early times, especially in towns, the Depression was very bad. There was no work anywhere, and migrants, not only Italians, but I speak of the Italians because they are the ones I know. They weren't allowed to speak their own language amongst themselves. Most of them would be walking along the street and people would yell out, "Oi you bloody dago, why don't you speak English?!"

That is what you got.

Did you get that personally?

No, not me, but …

Because you were in the country?

Yes. During shearing time, there were 10-12 shearers and all together about twenty extra men working. They have their own chef, you know, in a big hut with a dining room. They had their own stove there and a chef who used to cook for everyone. But, of course, that niggling thing about being Italian, being a *dago*, being this and that, you know. This meant that of course I was on my own, I couldn't go very much against the whole of them.

They were all Australians?

They were all Australians. But amongst them, there were always some good ones. Anyway, what happened, I will go back a little bit …

With the men that I used to work with at Noble's, they got to know me and to respect me, except one fella.

Were the men at Noble's all Australians?

Yes, they were very nice. They used to ask me about Italy, particularly the sons of this Bill that I was telling you about. They'd ask about Italy and what we had in Italy and one thing and the other. In the beginning, I was getting a bit cheeky. They were asking me what the spaghetti was and what it was like.

"Oh," I said, "it grows like willow trees and then they get long enough, we go along with the scissors, and we cut them."

"Oh!" They looked at each other.

When they found out I was having them on, well, you can just imagine. When I told them, they were made with flour, and you know ...

What year is this?

This was 1930-1931. The woolshed ... I was young (17-18) and strong, so they put me on the press. The press consisted of a square bag. The wool bag went into a box and what you did was you filled it up with wool and then you stamped it down, as tight as possible. Then, there was another box, and this box had bars on the bottom. You filled that up with wool and pressed it down. Then, what you did was with a pulley, you wound this on top of the other and removed the pins. On top, you put the lead and the lead has a bracket of steel across it. You put two steel ropes, one in each hook. Then you had a lever and put all the wool from the second one into the first one, and sometimes you had to press 400 pounds ...

Of course, I used to feel strong, I didn't mind. That built me up ... Ah! These shearers, used to say, "Let the little Italian do it! He is strong."

They had a wool classer, and this wool classer was the highest paid of the lot. He used to get twenty pounds a day! He came from Sydney and was a bit of a 'know it all'. He told the shearers and everyone else that he used to train for boxing. The shearers used to say to him, "What are you talking about boxing for? You couldn't beat that little Italian there. The little *dago* there." This kept going on daily, day after day, back and forth. After a while, they (the shearers) decided they would organise a spar between the wool classer and me. Me and the wool classer! He was supposed to be a boxing trainer for some boxer or something.

I said, "All right, okay, okay, okay." But I wanted the boss there to watch me. I trusted Mr Noble, and I never had put the gloves on before.

So, you actually had gloves and everything, with everyone around?

Oh yes, the shearers and everybody else were around. Oh yes, and this fight was to happen where we pressed the wool, on the table where the grading of the fleeces took place.

Anyway, the boss was sitting on this table with his watch. He decided that we'd have three rounds of three minutes. I thought, *Well, three minutes is not very long* ... but I tell you what, those three minutes happened to be the longest three minutes of my life.!

Anyway, it started off, and he came at me, and he hit me a few times. I nicked him, but not effectively and he cut back again hard ... and it was supposed to be a friendly spar. The first round went along in this way.

During the second round, I woke up to myself and I thought that I'd better do something here because otherwise … so I let him have a few. And he got really mad.

Anyway, the third round comes along, and he started off from over there and he comes like a bull. I stopped him and he threw punches, and I defended myself and I whacked him out, a left and a right. And you know what? After the right, I finished up throwing him underneath the table the boss was sitting on. He came out, and he said, "Oh! You hit too hard."

Well, he ended up with black eyes and he had the runs. You should have heard the shearers. "Oh, there goes our boxing trainer, there goes our boxing trainer. Oh, you really gave it to him, aye?"

Did things change after that with you and the shearers?

Oh yes, all the shearers thought that I was a great fella. It finished up that this wool classer couldn't stand it anymore, all the jeering and teasing, so he left. But before he left, he came to me and said, "You know, you can box, you have got a good reach, and you are strong. How about you come to Sydney with me, and I will train you as a boxer?"

I replied, "Oh no, you're kidding; not me, thank you very much."

That was it, he went, and they had to get somebody else to do the job.

This was in the very early years; Jack Lang[7] was the premier of the state, and the Harbour Bridge[8] wasn't completed.

---

[7] Jack Lang 1876-1975, Labor Premier of NSW 1925-27, 1930-32.
[8] The Sydney Harbour Bridge was opened in 1932.

So, during this time, you kept doing different jobs, going back and forth on properties?

Yes, and all the time on the sheep station. All the time employed under the Nobles. From there, the Nobles got into financial difficulties, and they decided that he had to give me the sack, to dismiss me.

Between 1930 and 1935, where was your father?

My father was at Wardell's at Mount Erin. He went to where my uncle was because in 1929, my uncle left for Italy. He went back because his wife would not come out to Australia.

Did he take much money home with him?

Oh yeah, he used to work at Lithgow on the steelworks and they used to pay him in gold pounds, and he saved up some money. At home, he had a good bit of land, which was independent of his wages. Anyway, he went to Italy and my father took his place, so he came closer to me then, closer to the Nobles.

How often did you see him?

Oh, quite often. Every fortnight, even every week, sometimes. I used to ride over there, and he used to ride over to me.

Did you know what was happening in the world, at the time? Did you hear anything?

Well, at those times, there was a lot of trouble in Italy. There was fascism, and there was some fighting in Spain after Germany went to Poland.

Going back to Merriwa, when I was dismissed from the Nobles, I went to work at Brindley Park. In the meantime, my father decided to leave Roach, and he came and stayed with me for a while. From there he moved to Sydney, to Smithfield, and that is where he bought the five acres.

When you were working at Nobles, what were you and your father aiming to do? What was the aspiration?

Oh well, Dad was thinking of going to Italy as well, and he would say, "How can I leave you here on your own?"

You see? So, he said, "I don't know … if I go to Italy, will you promise to be in contact with me, to write to me, write to your mother, and all the family?" All this was going on and on all the bloomin' time; he was really concerned, and he didn't want to leave me here on my own.

So he was thinking about going home?

Yes, he was considering going home or buying some land. It was a big decision. So, he finished up, when he came to Sydney and he met Chiarotto, who was from our same town, who we knew very well. And this fellow bought some land in Smithfield, and he told Dad that there was some land for sale there. So, Dad came down, and he bought it!

How much was it?

It was five acres of land for about 300 pounds with a bit of a humpy on it. Myself, I finished with Nobles. They wanted to make me a boundary rider, but they thought that I was too young and that it would have been a very lonely life for me. I would be in the saddle, every day of the week, riding around the fences and boundaries. As a boundary rider, I would have had to look after the crossings and the creeks and all the fences, where the water comes from the hill, fixing the fences and everything else. Well, Mr Jack Noble gave me a trial to see what I was capable of doing and he was satisfied that I could do the job, but Mr Noble, the old fellow, didn't agree. So, I had to leave.

I left Merriwa and came down to Smithfield because my father requested my help on the land.

When was the first time you heard that he was buying land in Smithfield?

Well, he talked about it a lot, but he bought the land in 1933. He talked about the possibilities of buying the land for a long time. While he came and stayed with me for a while, he was thinking about going to Italy or buying land.

What finally made him buy it?

He decided to stay in Australia, as he didn't want to leave me on my own.

And you weren't going back?

No, there was no hope of me going back. I said that when I left, "I'm to stay for four or five years at least and then I would come back again." But that is child's talk, you know, things didn't work out that way.

I wanted to stay. And I went to Smithfield. While in Smithfield, I got to play football.

Were there many Italians?

No, I was the only Italian in the football team. I always wanted to be a part of what was going on, I wanted to be part of Australia, I wanted to be part and parcel of everything. Although I always loved my country, I was always going to do the right thing in Australia. I wanted to show that I was an intellectual, that I was intelligent enough to appreciate the opportunities that I had and the way of life in Australia. Everything seemed to blend in together and I joined a football team. We played, but about three quarters through the season, my team got disqualified.

Why?

There were some fights and arguments about different things with different clubs. I wasn't involved in it; I only knew about it at the next meeting. I couldn't understand English very well, but enough to understand that the team was disqualified and was abandoned. We weren't allowed to play anymore because of what they said and what they did.

At this time, my dad and I started talking about asking to see whether Louie, my brother, cared to come to Australia.

Louie is the next son after you?

No, he is the third down. He accepted our proposition and came to Australia. He came to Smithfield.

When was that?

I can't be that accurate. I'll have to look at the dates. This must have been about 1933. Anyway, the three of us were cooking for ourselves.

What was it like to have Louie back?

Oh, it was fantastic. Everything that Louie and I did, it was in competition. When we put different plants in, we would get a row each and, of course, I had to be the first one to get out and he wanted to beat me. All of this you know! And we would do everything together, cooking and everything.

How many years younger than you was he?

He was three years younger.

Louie and I had some terrific times and arguments. Dad would go to the markets with things, and we would be left at home. The things that we used to get up to is nobody's business!

How was your brother with your dad? Because it would have been five years since he saw his father, if not longer?

Well, Dad left in 1927, for a few months, just to go and see his mother, and the family of course, and Louie arrived in 1933 …

So, what was their relationship like?

Well, their relationship was all right, but Louie always had been a very strong character. He believed in what he believed, and believed in what he wanted to implement despite what Dad or I said. He was strong in that way. He had a lot of common sense and was a terrific worker. He used to apply what he believed efficiently, and of course, I used to confer with him too. Sometimes, he used to go against my father's wishes with the way of doing things.

After a while, we decided to get Mum and my two brothers, Terry and Chana out.[9] Davino was still in college studying to be a missionary priest.

I remember Dad anticipating that we would have the two younger boys and so we would need some milk, so he decided to buy a cow. Then, he also wanted to buy a car; he bought a Fiat; a big Fiat! It was a huge thing, a seven-seater, with velvet seats, dickey seat; you should have seen it!

Was it brand new?

No, it was a second-hand one. The car was imported to take the prime minister and the bishops around and, you know, things like that. He got it cheap enough. He wanted to go

---
[9] Tarcisio and Luciano.

to the port and pick up Mum in a car. That was his pride, you know. We all concurred with his pride; we were like, "Yeah, okay, all right!"

So, the fact was even though we had a car, we were wondering if we could afford the petrol to go down there. It would have been about ten pounds of petrol and oil and some kind of bloomin' thing. It was expensive, oil ... we didn't know whether to cover that expense or have that money to go and get Mum because that was the only money that we had.

So, your father sent a letter to her, saying: "Look, it is time to come out, we have land now?"

Yes, all of these things ... well, he had to provide a house for her. He had prepared the bedroom, the bed, the curtains, we tried to do the right thing. Mum was really willing to come out. When she came here, you can just imagine the feast! The joy! We were all united except for Davino.

Terry and Chana, they went to school.

How old were they?

Well, they must have been about eight, nine, maybe even ten years old. They went to Fairfield Catholic School, and they used to help out in the farms when they got home from school. They had homework and everything.

Do you remember when they got off the boat?

Oh, we all went to meet them.

You ended up deciding to take the car?

We went to go and pick them up, the three of us in the car, the big car, the seven-seater. There were only six of us; there was room for another one.

What was it like when your Mum came off the boat?

Oh well, to describe that I would say I would need half a volume. The anticipation and the preparations! When Mum got off the boat, Mum and Dad were embracing. In fact, I didn't wait for Mum to get off the boat; I went on the boat. Dad tried to get on the boat, but he didn't sneak in; he wasn't as quick as I was.

Did she look different?

Oh no, not very much. Mum always had a very good complexion, anyway … you can just imagine. On the way home, we stopped for a drink.

What were your parents like?

When Mum came off the boat, my parents just talked. They loved each other, but they were a bit shy to do any embracing or kissing in front of us, except when we were first in town and then after it was never visible, anytime. There used to be a corridor between their bedroom and opposite it was my bedroom, and I could hear what was going on. The laughing and the joking and things like that. It was great. Everything was fantastic. We were all together, except Davino. Things were back to normal. From then on, we had proper meals cooked, very tasty, very good, you know. There was not one time without salt or another without this or another. Oh!

That was a great time. Terry and Chana used to go to school and Louie, and I, used to work in the farm. Dad was busy with the markets. Going to the markets, he had to get a carrier and sometimes, to avoid the expenses of the carrier, he had a big cart and a horse. We would load this cart up with vegetables and he used to pull the cart to Parramatta markets, in western Sydney. He did that for quite a number of years.

It would have taken him a long time to get there.

Well, he used to get up early enough to get to the markets with a horse and cart. That was life in those days; can you see how hard it was? But despite the duress and the hardships we used to go through, we were 'happy as Larry', all the time.

You know, we were lucky if we had two pence to go to the pictures some Saturdays. We used to walk to Fairfield to save the bus fare; yet all of these things built up character and my values. You've got to understand these things. It is not very easy for a young grown-up today with everything at your disposal… it is a different thing altogether.

I am grateful, to see the opportunity, to see that my grandchildren are here today, that they don't have to go through the hardships that I went through. When I arrived here, the boss where Dad was working told Dad to send me to school (and I would have to go ten miles to go to school). Dad said, "I can't send you to school. We have debts to pay. We have your trip, the house in Italy, and everything else." So, I had to work and earn some money. I gave every cent to my father until I was married, until I was twenty-seven.

So, the land that your father bought, and the house, it was yours as well?

It was my money, but it was a common family affair. When Mum arrived, I could see that the land was what it was — it was the family's. But I did think, that with Mum and the boys here, I would go back to Merriwa.

Why?

Because there wasn't enough to do at home for all of us. I thought, I've been working for so long and I needed some money. I would do better if I was in Merriwa earning some money privately. And things like that.

Did you like Smithfield at that stage?

Oh, I liked Smithfield. I liked Smithfield because of what it was giving, not that there was anything there. You know, we only had ourselves, we only had football meetings and sometimes there were parish meetings at the church, but I wasn't involved.

Also, my English wasn't proficient enough to participate in so many things. I used to help with manual things, cleaning up the church and things like that. Mowing and trimming the grass, keeping the place tidy and things of that nature. Apart from that, in the town itself, we had the garage, which was run by the Money's. Sam Money used to play football. There was Norm McCloud, he used to play football with me. There were others too, Jeff Stein.

So, I went to Merriwa, and I arrived there without a job. They said, (at Brindley Park) they would have a job for me because I was there before. I went there, and I got a job as a gardener. I did the chores, and sometimes, I would go out in the paddocks with the men, breaking in horses, riding horses, and things like that. This was at Brindley Park. The manager was Telfer. Brindley Park used to be a parcel of land, a grant of land given to Brindley, McCloud, and Fairfax. There was a million acres. These three divided it between themselves, and the part that I was working on was called Brindley Park.

Brindley Park itself could have been a couple of hundred thousand acres. Anyway, there was a lot to do there. They had horses and fat stocks, lambs, calves, everything going. While I was there, I got to know a fellow that used to play football and he used to go into training for one thing or another. But he was a 'pommy', an Englishman; he was a bit selfish in a way because he never asked me to go into town, go training, or anything like that, but he enjoyed having me play football (Rugby League). He was nice and everything, but he never put himself out. So, you know what I used to do? From Brindley Park, I used to run all the way to Merriwa for training. Then, I used to run back. And the distance could have been about eight or nine miles. I played football there. Anyway, after a while it happened that our team challenged the Upper Hunter Cup.

The Upper Hunter Cup was won three times by Murrurundi, so we challenged them; there was a competition. There was a special train that was assigned to take people from Merriwa to Murrurundi. The team and the whole bloomin' town got in their cars and on to the train and went to Murrurundi. Of course, we won it.

What was the score?

If I can remember, it was 24-14.

So, you can just imagine, after beating Murrurundi, there were fights from the football field to the station, and there were all sorts of things. They were really annoyed. Their trainer was a national footballer by the name of Ray Steer.

In the same year, 1934, Charles Kingsford Smith took a trip to country towns and took people for a joy ride for ten shillings a go.[10] This was to raise money to buy a plane to fly from America to race from England to Australia. He was a guest of Brindley Park. The Brindley Park property stretched right into the town; there was a fence, and that is where he landed with the plane. I was commissioned to get four bales of hay on the ute (utility) and go in this paddock and put one bale in each corner and light it up to give the wind direction to Kingsford Smith for his landing. Blimey, when I got there, he was already there! He had got there before me. I never had to light the bales. I took him up to Brindley Park for dinner.

What was he like?

Very few words, no jokes, a smile — yes and no. He answered the questions; he didn't ask too many questions. He was a solitary type of person. Then, he offered me a flight without paying that was worth ten shillings. So, I flew with him, in the Southern Cross.

I must say this, to my regret, that after that flight, I swore that I was never going to put my foot on another plane, because the thing came across air pockets and that was my first flight. The plane used to drop and go putt, putt, putt, putt. There were some other fellows there, and we both turned blue and then white.

This was your first time on a plane, and you flew with Kingsford Smith?! What was it like seeing the ground from up above?

I didn't get the time to see anything. I was concentrating on holding my stomach. I did see a bit, but that wasn't the thing that was worrying me.

---

[10] Charles Kingsford Smith (1897-1935) made the first transpacific flight from United States to Australia. He also made the first non-stop crossing of the Australian mainland. Sydney's airport is named after him.

From when you arrived in Australia to when your family reunited, did you feel you were missing out on anything as a young man because you didn't go to school? Did you feel you were missing out on anything?

Oh no, in fact, I always had an ambition to be useful in life. Where I worked and whatever I did, I always gave my all. Everything I had, I put in. With football on the field, where I worked, with whatever I was doing. I always had the ambition and desire to assert myself and to be accepted as an Australian and as a human being, as someone who was intelligent and capable.

On many occasions, when I was in Merriwa in particular, I was only young, but there were grown-ups that would do certain things in my presence, and I didn't think they knew what they were doing. So, I had to show them the way to do it. It was embarrassing to them, but nevertheless, the job got done.

I will give you an example. At Merriwa with the Nobles, we were fixing this terrace with new posts, and the terrace was huge with wisteria. They were trying to get the new posts underneath, but to get the new posts in, they had to pull the old ones out. I said nothing, and they were trying … so I went and got a chain and an old pole and another one in front and I tied the chain around the post (laughter) and one of them I levered so that I lifted it. I levered it up, by myself.

I used to be hated by the men because I knew how to do it, and they resented me knowing so much.

What do you think you learnt about yourself at that time?

What I learnt was that I was in my glory, and I was very happy that I was accepted. For instance, the majority of the people that I came in contact with accepted what I told them. I used to deliberately tell them what was going on in Italy, the way things were done in Italy, and what we had in Italy; the poverty, but also the wealth of things and the difference of the life and living. I would always finish up by saying, "One thing we never had was the pleasure of seeing such beautiful open spaces and sky and things." Australians used to gloat about that.

You arrived in Australia at fifteen, and then your father bought the land in 1932; these are some really important formative years for anyone. What did you learn about your then, that you still think about now?

I believed in my father and what he was doing. I recognised that he needed my help to do everything, and I knew that by helping him, that my mother, and the rest of the family could come to Australia. I applied myself entirely to saving and skimping in order to have 100 pounds in the bank, at the end of the year.

I used to mend my socks, patch my trousers, I used to wash everything and skimp with no resentment. I was so matter of fact. I was doing it, it was something to be done, and that was it. All of these bloomin' things put together ... I used to do it with love; everything I did, I was convinced that there as a purpose behind it all.

So, do you think that the love you had for your father and the total acceptance that you were there to help the family kept you going through all those years?

Apart from the football, I never had any other enjoyments. The only thing that I was extravagant on was to spend fifteen pounds to buy myself a motorbike. I saw the advert for it in *The Herald*, and I got Mrs Noble to ring up and send the money in. They sent it up to Merriwa. I took the bike to the mechanics. Mr and Mrs Noble told me to go and pick up the motorbike. Of course, I had never ridden one before, and I didn't know anything about a motorbike when I got to the garage to pick up the bike.

When I got there to pick up the motorbike, the mechanic asked, "Have you ridden a motorbike before?"

I said, "No!"

Then he asked, "So, how are you going to travel and take it home? There's twenty-five miles on the gauge and what about the creeks? Well, you better do a little bit of practice around the yard here." He had cars and spares parts around as I practiced. Finally, he said, "It's getting late, you better take off." So, I did.

I was going along, I had three gears—first, second and third. At first, I couldn't make it leave first gear. The engine was going faster and the bike slower, but bit by bit, I would get into the next gear. I got faster, and then I got to the next one, and that was really fast. By the time I got to the first gate, I knew a little bit about it and that would have been about fifteen kilometres from Merriwa. It took all that time for me to learn the function of the gears and everything. But I managed to get home with the motorbike.

When I got home, my wrists were aching, and my legs were sore because I was holding on like I was on a bucking bronco.

What an experience! Did you end up taking the motorbike back to Smithfield with you?

Yes, I took it back to Smithfield. I'll never forget when I left Nobles with the motorbike, as the thing wasn't going well. There was something wrong, and I had to get it towed with a rope. I had to keep one foot on the brakes and the other foot out so that I wouldn't get caught up in the rope and end up under the car. What a nightmare! From there, we managed to get it on the train to Smithfield and there we finally got it going.

Louie and I used to go out together, we had friends in Bossley Park, and we used to play *Bocce*.[11] We used to go to Liverpool and travel around to see friends on the motorbike.

---

[11] *Bocce* is an Italian bowling game, similar to bowls.

CHAPTER THREE
Making Smithfield Home

"So, I took Rina to the pictures.
She would have been sixteen or seventeen."

How long were you at Brindley Park before you came back to Smithfield again?

I wasn't there very long at all. In 1935, Dad wanted me home; I was twenty-two. While I was at Brindley Park, thirty acres of land came up for sale in Smithfield.

Dad wrote to me: "There is land for sale back in Sydney. If you agree and you tell me to buy it, I'll buy it, otherwise I won't." These thirty acres were in Smithfield. We had five acres, and these were an additional thirty acres in Woodpark Road. Nowadays, there are all factories on that land. I said, "Alright, you buy the land." The money that I earned, everything went towards the payment of that land.

How much was it?

I think it was about nine or ten thousand pounds.

That was quite a lot?

Yes, but it was thirty acres, you see. We could have made a fortune out of that. Millions. But that's beside the point.

Anyway, I came down to Smithfield, and I settled in to live with the family and we built a house on the thirty acres. While I was there, we bought another farm in Bourke Street, Smithfield, that was six acres. I don't remember how much we paid for that.

All of the places we had were on Prospect Creek. We used to pump water from it. The creek water used to come from

Prospect Dam; it used to be beautiful, clean water with fish in it, as well. Of course, that meant hard work.

What year did you buy the land on Bourke Street?

Bourke Street came after; it could have been 1937, but I forget now. To compensate for what I had done since coming to Australia, Dad gave me the land at Smithfield on Oxford Street. I got married there and built a small house that is still there now. That's where we got married and lived because the land was mine.

Oxford Street was built out to The Horsley Drive. Beyond that, there was the creek and grass. No bridge, no road. There was a waterhole at the end of the property which used to be called Little Manly because the kids used to swim in it.

What about Bourke Street?

Bourke Street was for the family. It was all for the family, until I got married, then what we produced in Smithfield was mine. Of course, Dad used to help and Chana, Terry, Louie — we all used to help each other. Louie ended up with Bourke Street. There was only a shed, and it was arranged to make it a comfortable dwelling. There was a kitchen and a bedroom, and that was where he started off his married life. Louie had married a girl from town, Rosina Recheia. They were furniture manufacturers. Louie was there for quite some time.

Did other members of the family migrate to Australia and live with you?

Yes, and originally, to start off, I found work for them. We got Davino out and Sante (my cousin) out. Before them, we got my cousins, John and Bruna Zadro, Richard, and

Frank's father, Genio, with his wife. I got a job for John and Bruna at a textile mill. I got a job for Gianinno at Recheia's. I got a job for Phil Zadro at another furniture manufacturer in Newtown.

I remember taking Phil over to the factory and the fellow there presented some plans and asked if he could read them. Phil said yes and explained what the plans were. "This goes here, that goes there." The boss said that he could start tomorrow. Genio went to work for the local council. Then, they got some land and started to produce some vegetables.

What was happening on the farm at this time?

On the thirty acres we had in Woodpark Road, we had to put in a pump. We wanted to put in an electric one. We had an electrical line from Kenyon Road across the properties. Louie, Dad, and me, we used to cut the trees, make the posts, dig the holes, and put them up.

Before we installed the pump in the creek, we never had a decent system, so we dug big holes and filled them with water using the pump. Then, using two large watering cans of ten litres each, we attached them to either side of a yoke that we used to water the plants with. It was 10,000, 20,000, 30,000 plants at a time—cauliflower, cabbage, etc. It was unbelievable. The ploughing was all done with two horses and a plough. We would hold on to the plough and walk up and down. On my property at Smithfield, I only had one horse and a small plough.

In 1937, Dad went to Italy by himself. After Mum arrived, Dad went back to see his mother, who used to live with Zio Emilio. Zio Emillio had come to Australia in 1925, and when he was here, John was born. Louie and I were left here, and

Mum took sick. We took her to different doctors, and she finished up in hospital, where she had a hysterectomy. We didn't say anything to Dad, so when he came back, we told him and he went crook, as if we had put a knife in his chest. He was away for three months.

What was your dad like, at this time?

Dad had a personality that was unique. When he returned to Italy, to visit his mum after many years, he travelled in a first-class cabin on the ship. His ability to talk, express himself, and joke, meant the sailors wanted him at their table, going there and coming back. When he came back, he invited a lot of the sailors for a shooting escapade, and they came to our place, and he took them shooting.

He also joined the Merrylands Bowling Club. Dad was responsible for the first championship won by Merrylands, and I have a photo with him and the other members who won the championship. I believe Dad's photo is still on display at Merrylands. He could never speak English well though, it was very broken.

He never spoke as well as you?

No. I could have done better too, if I had the opportunity to go to school. In fact, I'm getting worse with my pronunciation, due to age.

When the other members of the family started coming to Australia, what did they tell you of Italy? Of what was happening? Did you feel homesick when they were telling you the stories?

Yes. I always wanted to go back to Italy; always. You become curious. You ask questions like: "Where is so-and-so now?"; "How is so-and-so?"; "What happened with

...?"; and even, "Oh, they've built this and knocked down that."

Were there more Italians coming into the area?

Yes, from all over Italy, from the south to north.

This was all happening in the late 30s so, was the Depression starting to bite?

Yes, then there was the Depression.

What the council and the state did was, instead of giving the dole, they paid men to work so many days a week. So, what they did was dig in the creek (Blind Creek) at Smithfield that used to run parallel behind the park and the properties to town. It was all done by hand. There used to be 100 to 120 men working.

One would dig here, throw the dirt up to the next man, and then to the next one, who would have a horse and scoop it up and level the soil off. They used to work on a roster for their dole, for the money. It used to provide a means for a living to provide food, to keep horses, but it was very, very hard. It used to be depressing as a foreigner, to see that I was living much more comfortably than a lot of the Australians were. I am proud of what we did and achieved because I was in Merriwa working during the Depression. And that Bill East that I was telling you about, his sons were unemployed, and I was working!

So, you or your father were never really out of a job at all this whole time?

No, never. When I left Brindley Park to come home permanently, my boss, gave me a ham to take home to my father. He used to come around with me and put his arm around me. He was a big man, and he used to call me Frank. He was of German origin. He would give me commissions such as asking me to take the car and go to the woolshed to deliver messages, about five to six miles away, and to see so-and-so, and tell him to do this and this, etc. There was another Italian living where I worked, and he never had the opportunity that I had. Telfer never gave him the car or told him to do anything. Telfer had three daughters. The younger one, I could have done something there, but it was around Christmas, and Dad told me that I'd better go home, because we had the thirty acres going and they needed looked after.

At Telfer's, we used to kill the pigs, cure them, and make the hams ourselves. I was looking after all of this, with brine and salt, and we used to dry it with salt to pickle them. He gave me one to take home. Telfer said, "Enjoy this with your father." I think it was because I used to speak about my father, "My father this ... my father that ..."

Before Smithfield, my father was in Merriwa for a long time specialising in haystacks. In those days, when they had a lot of hay, they never had sheds to store it in, and the secret was to make these stacks waterproof. The stacks that Dad made could have been there for ten years and no water would get in it. He was noted for that. These farmers would talk about it. It was a skill he learned in Italy.

But back in Smithfield, bit by bit, we acquired hoses and pipes. We used to have water holes and use pumps to get the water up. Finally, we accumulated a bit of money, and I bought the Skinners Spray System. From the pump right down to the end of the farm, I bought the pipes and attached them to the posts and sprays. Skinners are pipes with holes and nipples that spray water out. Start the motor and open the taps, and all the watering was done. What an improvement!

While in Smithfield with Rina, this one-acre property on Oxford and Smithfield Road came up for sale. I knew the fellow who used to live there, Mr and Mrs Velli of Italian origin. Velli's father was a foreman for the waterboard when they built the canal.

I had the pleasure of knowing him. He was a very positive sort of man; he was fantastic to talk to. Velli's father spoke of his experiences, though in spite of all his experiences, he was never accepted because Australians only accepted themselves. It's like the Opera House. The architect that designed the Opera House was never accepted because he was a foreigner; he ended up leaving before it was completed.[12]

Anyway, that was how it was. Even with me, when I used to go out of my way to do something that was a little bit different or new, they never appreciated it. There was no thanks or sign of gratitude such as, "That was a good idea." Never!

Because you were Italian?

Oh yes, because I was a foreigner.

Did you have any Australian friends at this stage?

Yes, I had many good Australian friends.

But you were always a bit different because you were Italian?

No, my friends accepted me. I wanted to be accepted. If I said something, it wasn't to show off, it was to make things easier. But that was how it was in those days.

---

[12] The Sydney Opera House's architect was Jørn Utzon. He was Danish.

How did your father deal with the racism around at that time, especially being a man who was older when he came to Australia? How was his experience different to yours?

That is a very interesting question. Despite my father's limited knowledge of English, he was accepted fully because he displayed a level of intelligence with whatever he was saying. However, he didn't speak English well, for instance to say, "I beg your pardon?" Instead, he would say, "Pay punt?" (laughter).

But, he could make himself understood. There was an expression of a phrase he would apply in such a manner that you would have to accept it. He had personality.

And that was his gift?

Oh, for sure. For him to be accepted at Merrylands Bowling Club, was prestigious. He was the only Italian there, and he was accepted because of his character and ability to play sport. Even today, Australians value a person for their ability to play sport. That was something I could not claim, because I never had time to play. Like *Bocce*, even though it is played at the Club[13], I'm lucky if I've played two or three games. I played cards a little bit, but not in competition with anybody.

Because you didn't have the time?

When I was younger, my ambition was running, athletics, and long jump. When I had the opportunity in Merriwa, it was climbing hills and mountains. I'd go right up to the top and see as far as the eye could see because I thought I could see Italy. That nostalgia stayed with

---

[13] Club Marconi.

me for a while; it still is with me now, but not so much. You see how your children, grandchildren, and great-grandchildren blend in.

If your father's gift to being accepted in Australia was his personality, what do you think was yours?

With me, I wasn't as liberal as Dad was. Possibly, I was a little bit pretentious because I wanted to be recognised and to be accepted, and perhaps, it was too evident. When you press at something, it isn't as easy to be accepted. Don't you agree?

So, possibly that was my problem. I had lots of friends in football, and family friends. There were people who accepted me like Hector Behagg. Behagg and I were like brothers. He had the poultry farm along The Horsley Drive. He had two boys, and he used to come to our place, even the place we built when I got married.

Hector Behagg came from a very rich family. His brothers were solicitors, but he didn't want to study. He was a carpenter by trade, then he got married and bought himself a poultry farm. He had a motorbike, a Triumph, with which he used to come over on.

Dad had a horse, and it would start and stop when it wanted to, and Hector would come over and lead the horse. He entrusted me with his poultry farm when they went away. I had so many friends: the footballers, the Steins, the McNortons. No question about it.

Did you enjoy your life in Smithfield at this time?

Smithfield was home. I liked the people; we used to get along very well, and I had no enemies.

Through the Depression, the Italian community really multiplied and with no work, the Italians got to sharing land (renting and buying land) to grow vegetables to live and support their families. By doing this, they became very popular. There were a lot of Italians in the Fairfield area, and they all had farms, and were self-employed.

They helped with the progress of the district, no doubt about that. It was fantastic to go along to where they played bowls and you would meet someone and they would say, "Oh, you're from so and so? How are you?", etc.

Reminiscing about the past was a real pastime and the jokes we had! We also had the church and the life of the church and the CYO (Catholic Youth Organisation). Our children became members of the CYO. We were part and parcel of the church. We used to have picnics, and go swimming, going in the truck.

I, myself, have always been on committees. Most of the time, I was a chairman or president of a group promoting charities, promoting functions, and things like that in Smithfield. We were very successful, you know.

In Smithfield, we built a hall and church, we had a dance, a charity dance, and the amount of people who came was amazing. We didn't know where to put them! The Italian Consul came along to this function, and I had to do the honours.

First of all, I had to be presented and then I had to do the honours. I had to say, "This is the Consul so-and-so …"

He said, "But Zadro, how did you manage to get so many Italians together? We are grateful if we get a quarter of this for anything!"

I remember these words, you know. He was full of praise for the enthusiasm the people had. To promote and do things, to replace parts of the mass with an Italian sermon, things of this nature. It was fantastic.

It is so different now. In those days, we had a lot of migrants that could not understand the language. They really longed for an Italian mass and an Italian priest to give a sermon.

So they could understand and feel connected?

Yes! They were able to communicate with them and it was something fantastic to see how they cherished the coming of these missionaries. They used to be very scarce at one time.

The Smithfield story began with a little church built in the early 1800s, and they called it St Gertrude. What happened was, things got moving, and they got this Benedictine Father from America; in fact, two of them came. The first was from India, Father Farina. He was a humble person and a very nice priest. He was Catholic, but the Protestant Fraternity also loved him. When he left Smithfield, we gave him a farewell party. I was involved in all that business.

I remember the president who organised his farewell party. I used to play football with him, and of course, I was with him, and they wanted me everywhere!

That is what I cherished. I wanted to feel like one of the mob!

When this priest left, another Italian priest came along, Father Cletus. At this time, it was decided that we should have a Catholic school. What happened with the church was that they removed all the windows because they were arched and tall and all around. They removed them and took them away and made wider windows to make a classroom out of it.

It was a shame. I had the windows at my place for years and years, all made out of beautiful timber.

I had them because I was there all the time, and I had a truck for delivering stuff and taking stuff and all that sort of thing.

They said, "Please take them away — or clear them out. Take them to your farm. You have plenty of room up there."

So, I said, "Okay."

I held them up here with other things and I suggested we sell them, but they wondered who would want them. I tried to get interest with some of the cabinetmakers and construction people, but they didn't bother with them. So, they ended up in the fire. I got fed up with having them about.

Let's go back a little; tell me about how you first met Nanna.

Well, first of all, I must tell you that Nanna's father was a technology teacher in the Mechanics Field. When he came to Australia, there was no work for his trade. He had to humble himself to become a motor mechanic. He used to teach us how to use the appliances that were used in those days and all of these things. He was a teacher, and yet, he had to resort to motor mechanics.

We had a Fiat (which we talked about) and we thought that coming from Italy, he would be the man that knew the Fiat, inside out. My dad approached him about this Fiat and because it wasn't working, he picked him up with the truck and brought him back to my place. They got talking about the past and the First World War, and it turned out that they were in the same regiment!

We took the car to be fixed in Fairfield, and I went over to pick the car up. As I walked around to the side entrance of the garage, I looked through the window and there was a girl mopping the floor. She had her dress tucked under the bloomers, the ones that were tied with elastic at the knee and there she was, scrubbing the floor. After a good look, I kept going through to see her father.

Her father was in the garage and showed me around because I was inquisitive about his mechanical experiences. I have always been attracted to mechanics. He then insisted that I go inside. He was a very well-educated person. Not a word out of place, very polite and entertaining, and he introduced me to Rina. Rina had a sister, Maria, and a brother, Peter, and they requested that I visit with them again.

Louie tried to make a line for Maria, but Maria was already going with Leo, and Rina, well, I liked her very much. I was about twenty-six years old, and Rina was sixteen or seventeen years old. I kept going to see her there, and one day, I asked her to come to the picture show with me. I asked her mother if she would allow me to take Rina to the pictures in Fairfield.

"Alright," she said, "But you know what I expect of you."

I said, "Yes. I do know and I will respect your wishes. Don't worry."

So, I took Rina to the pictures; she was still a teenager. So, no kissing, nothing like that … Are you joking!?

Did you have a good time, and did you get along?

We got on alright. I took her home and her mother was waiting up for us.

After that, we decided we would organise a picnic because that is what I used to do. For years and years, I organised the Zadro picnics, and the Sesto picnics, for all the people from Sesto.

What was Rina like at this stage?

Oh ... a wild horse! Full of life!

She was outgoing! As I said, she was really into life. Horse jumping, climbing, anything. Full of life!

We went out and organised the picnic, and of course, I organised it because I wanted her and her sister to be with us. When we went out there, there would be cousins such as Sante. He didn't have his wife here then.

Rina would always pretend to be indifferent to me. I didn't exist! I was dying! I was driving the truck, and I was dying to have her in the cabin with me. Oh no, not in your bloomin' life! She would be out the back, laughing and joking with the rest of the boys. Just like that. A tomboy. This went on for quite a time. I thought to myself, *"Oh well, I can see that it was no good me wasting my time.* But I always had her on my mind.

It finished up that I met up with Amy Vassallo and her younger sister. The sister was fair, and Amy was dark. Two beautiful girls. Of course, another two Italians approached the father of Amy, and they used to laugh and joke because the father never allowed them near the two girls. They never had a chance with her father protecting his girls.

Oh, I'll see about that, I thought, and I called around to their place. I met the father, and he asked me inside. So, I decided to take Amy to the pictures, but her mother had to come with us. Bit by bit they got to know me, and they trusted me.

I took Amy to the pictures in Fairfield. When we came out of the pictures, we saw Rina, and Amy said she knew that I had been making a line for Rina. To make Rina jealous, Amy went up to speak with her. When Rina saw me with Amy, she was taken aback, and I thought, *Hello there*. So, I kept pursuing Rina, and I broke it off with Amy; these were for other reasons, as well.

Rina's sister, Maria, liked me, and she really went out of her way to make arrangements for Rina and I to meet and to be together. One Saturday, we made an appointment to meet at Rina's house and go to the pictures. Inside the house, there was another fellow's parents talking to Rina's mother and father. They had gone to Rina's place with their only son, and he took Rina to the pictures. This was a stab in my heart.

What did you do?

Well, I suffered, of course. It hurt.

Did Rina's family tell you that she went to the pictures with this man?

Oh, yes.

And what did you say?

I couldn't say anything but, "We were supposed to go to the pictures together!"

They said, "Oh, we're very sorry, but we didn't know anything about that!"

This Bill guy was from a family they knew, and the son had expressed his interest in Rina. They tried to do their best to make it work by going over to see the Spinelli family (Rina's family) with their son. He took Rina to the pictures, and they were waiting for them to come home, so I waited with them.

When they arrived, Rina said, "Oh, hello."

"We were supposed to go to the pictures together," I stated.

She denied she knew that these plans had been made with her sister, Maria, who was out with Leo and could not confirm the arrangements. Even to this day, she denies knowing. Anyway, after that she decided to go to the pictures with me.

So, she really didn't like this other fellow?

No, they were just friends. To her, they were just friends, and I believed it. She never had any feelings for him. Anyway, I took her to the pictures.

Leo had a utility, and he would come up and I would borrow the 'ute' and take it for a run around the place. In the cabin, Rina and I would stop and talk, but no kisses, nothing. One time I said, "Look Rina, you know how I feel about you. If you don't feel the same, say so now and we will call it quits."

She looked like she was in a trap, and she replied, "Oh, no."

"Well? Should we go together?"

"Yes," she nodded, and we had our first kiss.

How did you court one another?

We used to be the same platonic way. We did a bit of smooching, very conservative, no mucking around.

Did you go to the movies?

Yes. We would go for ice cream, and we might hold hands, but that was as far as it went, and that was not too easy either. It took a long time before that was even acceptable or permissible.

Tell me the story about the time you tried to touch Nanna's hand, and she wouldn't let you.

I can't remember the specific time, but I tried so many times, it's not funny. She used to get so indignant.

This one time, we went for a picnic up the mountains with Leo and Maria (with his vehicle). We decided to stop on the side of the road and go into the bush a bit. Leo and Maria were engaged and used to smooch about while Rina and I went walking about the bush and finished up sitting on a log. Rina was sitting lower than I was and I was stroking her hair. That was alright, she allowed me for a bit, she wasn't nasty or anything about it.

The next week, I went over to see her, and she told me, "Oh, just as well you come. I don't want to see you anymore."

I was dumbfounded. "What happened? What did I do?" I asked.

"You know what you did! Who do you think you are taking liberties?"

Strike a light! "You must be joking?" I retorted. "I didn't think anything of it. I thought it was very nice and pleasing. What do you think I think of you?"

She thought I thought she was easy.

How long did you go out together for?

It was a while. A couple of years.

And then you decided to get married?

Yes.

Was this something you had discussed a lot?

We knew. I said, "We're talking about marriage now … you know what happens, don't you?" She used to work in a factory, at the time.

"I'll work in the factory," she advised.

I replied, "You'll become a farmer's wife. Not that I expect you to do much on the farm, but that is what you'll be. Do you realise that?"

"Oh, yes," she nodded.

She wanted that. And we finished up in a little home.

How and where did you ask Nanna to marry you?

I think it was in her house one day; it was one evening, a Saturday or Sunday. I used to go there twice a week (to her parents' house).

Did you ask her father first?

It was a funny thing. Her father got sick before anything happened and he died before we got married. Maria already had her engagement, so she went ahead and got married, but the wedding was played down a little bit.

At Rina's father's funeral, the Australian flag was at half-mast and a man in uniform was standing to attention when the cask went past. He used to write music for and play in a Fairfield band. He played for the opening of the Harbour Bridge.

His name was Edwardo Spinelli; he was a very nice person. When he got sick, the stroke impaired his speech. I could understand what he meant and what he was trying to tell me—to look after his little Rina. He used to love Rina. "Look after her and cherish her."

Her mother said to me, "I don't know why you want to marry Rina, Felice. She'll be no good to you. She's not used to a hard life."

"Well, it's up to her to decide," I replied.

Her response was, "Well, I know you and your family and it's just as well that I do, otherwise I don't know if I would allow this."

It must have been a hard time for her losing her husband so young?

Of course, it was difficult after the loss of a loved one and when we were on the farm, Rina's mother would come and visit us and she was happy, because Rina was happy.

What Rina would do to help was incredible! I had to stop her. We did things together all the way. She helped me on the farm, with accounts, and with everything, and I helped with the children where I could.

To make matters worse, we had built a house and had the electricity installed, but we couldn't get it connected because it was in the war years and council didn't have the wires. They never had anything, and we spent a few years even without any hot water. We had a copper, which we would boil with wood, and we used to get the water with a bucket from the copper and pass it through the window into the bathroom. We had a veranda with the bathroom window and a laundry located further up with the copper.

Were children something you both wanted straight away?

Children? We were three months married and Rina says, "I want a baby."

"Alright, it'll come. We'll have a baby," I replied.

A couple of weeks or days go by, and she still says, "I want a baby!"

The baby finally did come, and she was very happy and proud. She used to walk beside me with this big tummy, proud as punch.

Did you and Rina always want the same things out of life? For example, were children something you both wanted straight away?

Well, I must say that I was very fond of music. In fact, I had a few lessons with a violin, but I could not pursue it. This was when I was in Merriwa. I will tell you about a fella I knew there. There was an old chap there, by the name of Fred French. He had a fiddle which he used to play, and he wanted me to learn. I learnt to play three songs. He'd say, "Keep going, you're doing alright." Fred was a character; he had white hair and a moustache, a real bushman.

There were such stories he used to tell me about the bushrangers and especially Jimmy Governor.[14] Once they

---

[14] Jimmy Governor was an Indigenous Australian who married a white woman, Ethel Page, in 1898. He and his brother, Joe, were known as the last known outlaws of New South Wales. They killed nine people and went on armed rampages.

went to look for Governor, there were about ten men, and he said, "I did see him, and he did see me, and I got arrested. I turned around and went the other way." He wasn't a gangster; he was just ill-treated. In those days, there was slave labour for the English.

Anyway, Fred used to camp and trap. He used to follow fences, find a hole they had made, and trap rabbits and foxes and things. You know I told you about a man who took me to Simpson for work and he took me to the doctors in town? Well, this old gentleman who played the fiddle, used to camp at this site (and he used to trap around the hills and bush there). I knew he was there on his own.

Over Easter one year, he was on the site by himself, so I picked up some lettuce, beans, and vegetables that I had grown in my garden, and I rode over and gave him some. You should have seen that man. The joy and look of appreciation. He said to me, "By crikey, it took an Italian to think of me!"

When shearing time came, he used to do some shearing himself and entertain the shearers with his violin and that's where I got to play.

Is that something you would have liked to have pursued?

Oh, I would have liked to very much, but we were twenty-five miles from anywhere. He knew I was up there on my own during those holidays, so he came up from Merriwa to visit me.

I had the keys to the hut, and I let him in. Inside was a stretcher, and he brought his things and slept there. He thought the world of me, and he said, "I knew that you would not do any wrong and it's not fair that a young man like you, a young kid, should be up here on his own." He had come over to keep me company.

He used to drink rum, and of course, whenever he used to drink, he would want me to have one. I couldn't drink like he did, but he was in my hut drinking and when it came time to go home, he took off in the wrong direction. "Fred," I called, "that way, that way!"

He got cranky and shouted, "What!! You're telling me how to get home?"

"Fred, don't get annoyed. Look, you stop and think, and you'll see this is the right way."

"By crikey, you're right!" He agreed after a minute, and he made his way home.

One day, I didn't see him, and I wondered if he was alright. I went over to his hut, and he had colic. I said, "What's the matter Fred? What's the matter with you?"

"I opened a tin of sardines," he moaned. "I ate a tin of sardines, and this is what … oh, blimey!"

"You know what? Castor oil will fix that."

"You think so?" He almost pleaded.

"Well, I can't think of anything else." So, I went and got the castor oil because I had it all the time and I gave him a good dose of castor oil with milk in it and that fixed it.

Later on, he got sick with a hernia, and he was taken to hospital in Merriwa. One day, I got a lift into town with the boss on a Saturday. They used to do the shopping on a Saturday, and I went to see Fred in hospital. You should have seen that man. When he saw me, he had tears rolling down his face. "Oh, you thought of me," he said. "God bless you!"

Of course, sometimes I think of these happy souls and this man. He was a real bushman. He wasn't a religious man, but his principles and his values, would beat any religion. What a man. I then heard he passed away, and I thought about how he never even gotten married. That was Fred French.

CHAPTER FOUR

Building Community and a New Home

"It takes a good Italian to be a very good Australian."

Nonno, how did WW2 affect you and the family?

The Second World War was, by now, in full swing with the Allies, and all foreigners became enemy aliens.

How did that happen?

That happened legally. The Australian authorities took precautions with the migrants that were here, as they thought they could be a threat to the security of the country. This wasn't completely wrong, but we were all interned.

Before you were interned and all the migrants were made enemy aliens, how did people that you knew, that you dealt with daily at church or at work, act towards you? Did they change?

Oh no. The public, the people that we knew or knew us, were amazed that they (the authorities) thought it was necessary, but the fact is this—the military authorities (apparently, they were English), went around and rounded up all the migrants.

One day, they called in at my cousin's place and questioned every one of us about our politics, our way of living, what we thought of England, what we thought of Australia, and what we thought of the war. They went through the house looking for things that might incriminate us. The person doing the questioning happened to be Ray Steer.

Ray Steer was an international footballer who played for Australia. Of course, when I heard his name, I asked him, "Have you coached the Merriwa team?"

"Yes," he stated. "How did you know?"

I told him that I had once played for Merriwa and that we had beat Murrurundi for the Cup. I told him about the train ride back to the station and how we weren't very popular with the locals.

But anyway, when Mr Steer got to know about me playing football, he was very pleased. He was really a different person altogether. He said, "Come with me, we'll go down to the police station in Smithfield."

While we were there, I got talking with the police officer because I knew him very well also. We used to have to go there to get petrol coupons. Also, when we would go into town and around where I lived, we would meet with each other.

Anyway, Mr Steer advised, "Well, Phil[15], you are not to worry. You and your family are decent people. You don't have anything to worry about." So, I was very happy about that.

A little while after, things started to change. The next thing there was a call up of all enemy aliens, for Labour Corps. The ones that were called up had to go for a medical examination. That is when I went to Merrylands; they had a big hall there. I was very sorry to leave. I had to leave my wife in the condition that she was in. She was expecting our

---

[15] Phil was the name Felice was mostly called by family and friends. Many people thought his name was Phillip. This was an Anglo-English interpretation of Felice. The closet English translation of Felice is Felix.

first child and in her last few moments of the pregnancy. I thought, *Well what can I do about it?*

Let's go back a bit Nonno; so, in the end, you were called up?

Yes, the week after I had met with Ray Steer, I went to Merrylands to buy *The Herald* newspaper on my push bike. I rode there and came back. On the way back from Merrylands, down Kenyons Road, there was one car after the other and they all finished off turning to the right, turning towards Horsley Park, Wetherill Park, Bossley Park, and so on. At this sight, I began to wonder what was taking place.

I got home, and I sat down with my wife. I started to read the paper to see whether there were any jobs, whether there was something that could be done because there was a terrible drought and there was no water. The creek, it was bone dry. I could walk with my slippers on the bottom of it. I couldn't grow anything under the circumstances, so I was looking to get a job.

The next thing, there was a knock at the door. When I answered the door, there were two fellows, both well-dressed, and they asked me my name. I told them who I was and one of them said, "You have to come with us."

"Oh? Whatever for?" I asked.

"It is not our duty to answer any questions," they stated. "We were told to come and pick you up and you have to come with us."

"And where are we going?"

"Oh," they said, "Exactly where, we don't know, but we have to take you to Guildford."

I shook my head. "Oh, no! Look, under the circumstances, I cannot leave my wife as she is."

"Oh, but you must," they replied.

There was one thing discussed and we went back and forth.

We went through the doors into the house. I had a camera that was given to me as a wedding present from my brother and they took it. They couldn't find anything else, so they kept insisting that I had to go with them.

"Be reasonable," I pleaded. "How could I leave my wife under the circumstances? She is expecting at any moment. I can't leave her here like this!"

"Well, we understand your predicament, but we have to abide by our orders," they insisted. "You have to come with us."

"I'll tell you what we'll do," I replied. "We pick up my wife and we take her over to my mother's. I'll come with you, but we go and drop my wife off with my mother and then I'll come with you."

"Oh, we can't do that! We can't deviate from where we are," they replied.

"Look," I declared, "I'm not coming with you."

We were getting a little bit heated up. Not only them, but myself and my wife who, by now, was crying. That didn't avail to anything though, as they were refusing everything.

By chance, my father called around on his way back from the markets with his truck. He was anxious to see Rina because she was expecting and anxious to see the new baby - he was a real family man. So, it finished up that my wife went with Dad, and I went with the two men.

I finished up at this hall with another two or three fellows that I knew. They had separated us with a gate and a table was set up. On top of the table was a book and, in the book, there was a list of names. I could see the name of my father and my brother and a score of people that I knew from Smithfield, Wetherill Park, and Bossley Park. While I was looking at this, an officer saw me, and he reprimanded me, and he told me to get inside.

They decided to take us to Liverpool. In Liverpool, there was a military camp, and we occupied one of the rooms. There were four of us in this room, and so we began the interns' life.

All meals were provided, and we just had to look after our room and everything like that. As it was during the time of the drought, they decided that we should build a well. There were some concreters in the camp with us. There were about 200 or 300 of us there, all together.

So, who decided to build a well?

We decided. We suggested it to the authorities that we might be able to dig a well for water. Instead of making cylinders, because we never had the right equipment, we had to make diagonal ones. We started to dig, and we went down with these pipes, the diagonal ones. They were about four feet each in height and about five feet in diameter. We started to dig, and I volunteered for the job, because I was getting bored, and so we made this well. We struck rock and we couldn't dig anymore, so it was left there, it was abandoned.

After days of digging and trying to occupy myself, I got word that I had a son!

How long after did this happen?

Well, it was not long after that because I was interned at the beginning of April and Joseph was born on 20th April 1941.

I thought to myself, *I wonder if they will let me see my wife and my baby?* I approached the major and asked him. He didn't say no, but he said, "Let me think it over."

Not so long after, I was called, and he said, "Yes, tomorrow you can go and see your wife in Fairfield Private Hospital, but you have to be accompanied by a soldier."

"That's okay," I replied and added, "no worries."

So, the next day, a sergeant with a rifle accompanied me. He escorted me to Fairfield. To get there I had to catch a train, and I felt very embarrassed to be sitting there with him. Nevertheless, I was very happy to be going to see my wife and my son!

We got off at the station at Fairfield and not far from the exit of the station, there was a hotel. This sergeant said to me, "Phil, where is the hospital?"

"Over there, see that building? That is where the hospital is."

He said, "Look, I am going in there for a drink. You won't do anything silly, will you?"

"No," I promised. "I assure you I won't do anything silly. I'll go and see my wife and after, I'll come back here and pick you up, and we will go back to Liverpool."

Instead of me picking him up, he came over to the hospital and met my wife and child.

What happened when you saw Nanna?

To describe that moment would take a book in itself, I think.

To see my own child and everything! There was Rina, Dad, and there was little Joey in her arms. There are no words to describe the joy but also the anxiety about not being with her to care of them. Instead of staying with them, I had to go back to the internment.

Who was looking after Nanna, at that point?

At that point, her mother and my mother took care of her and little Joey. They used to share the caring for her. I was there about an hour, at the most, and then, I had to go back.

After a while of being interned, my wife began to feel better, and she came to see us.

She told me that a certain party in authority in Smithfield suggested to her that she should sell our property in Smithfield to him. He told her that the authorities were going to confiscate all foreign migrant property. I could mention the name of the person, but I would rather not. And besides, this person is now deceased, and his family is no longer in the area. He was in the police force; I will say that much.

Consequently, not long after that, he was demoted from his position. In the same token, I knew a friend of mine that gave some money to the same police officer, and they were not interned. He had that much authority.

When I went to get the petrol coupons, he used to say to me, "Don't forget Phil, I have got tremendous power."

I didn't bite. I just congratulated him and said, "Very good." Ha!

Did you believe what Nanna had told you? That they were going to take your land away?

No, I didn't believe it. But I was worried it might be so because of the thousands of internees we had from all over Australia. But I would like to narrate an episode that happened during the internment in Liverpool.

One morning, we got up at the usual time and we heard some women singing some Italian songs. We thought, *Where would this be coming from?* They were women's voices, so we went towards the sound of the voices and there was a contingent of women, interned from Queensland. They were calling out, "What is wrong with all you men? Are you all dead?"

They were really cheerful, but instead of cheering us up, it depressed us, because we had never thought to see women interned.

So, they were in the next barracks, were they?

Yes, they were in the barracks next to us.

Soon after, the authorities decided to get a group of us and take us to Sydney to be seen before a judge at a court to find out what we really were.

Before you were moved, they said to you, "We are going to move you and you all have to go to court in the city."

Yes.

Had you heard any stories of anyone that had gone before you?

No.

Did you have any idea of what was going to happen?

No, we didn't know anything. We were really concerned, and we thought, *Are they really taking us to Sydney? To go to court?*

We got to William Street, I think it was, and they put us in a hall. There they told us to wait until we were called. One by one, we were called in and questioned. When my turn came, I went in, and I went before three judges and an interpreter. The interpreter spoke fluent Italian. They started to question me about when I came to Australia and when I was in Italy.[16] Was I a fascist? Of course, I wasn't. Then, they asked did I belong to the party?

"No," I declared.

"But how come?" They queried. "It was compulsory for everyone to belong to the party and not you?"

"Well, in my town, I belonged to the Catholic organisation and the mayor of our town, never, never forced anyone to join the fascist party. I never had to, I was never asked to, and I didn't bother."

The next question was, "But you love Italy?"

I said, "Yes."

Then, they asked me further questions about Italy, fascism, the war, Germany, and one thing and another. I said that all of those questions didn't interest me. They said, "How come? You love Italy!"

"Gentleman, I do love Italy, but I intend to respect this country and its laws, which have given me my life and

---

[16] The memory of the questioning is as Nonno remembered it.

allowed me to come and live here. The opportunity to come to Australia is one that I appreciate very much. I'm very grateful."

Did you answer those questions in English or Italian?

English.

So, the interpreter wasn't really needed?

No. Well, he spoke in Italian (the interpreter). He was saying, *"Do you fully understand it? Capice?"*

Then, I was asked questions about where I worked in Australia, where I'd been, and what I did. I told them I played football for Smithfield and Merriwa where I was in a stock station and sheared sheep for my bosses called the Nobles. There was a father and a son with his wife on the property. The father's wife was living in town with his daughter. All these questions!

They asked, "Do you think you can get a job in Merriwa? Where you worked before? At the Nobles?"

"Yes, it is quite possible that they would give me a job," I replied.

"Well," they said, "you write, and if they give you a job, we will release you."

I wrote to the Nobles. They sent back a reply and told me to come up to Merriwa with my wife so they could give me a job.

I told the Department of Enemy Aliens that the Nobles could only give me a job in Hampshire, twenty-five miles from Merriwa. I explained that there are fourteen gates to open and three creeks to cross. I said there was no running water, so how could I take my wife up there in the condition that she was in? They realised the problem and asked, "Is there anywhere else you could get a job?"

It so happened that my brother-in-law had a factory in Newtown; Leo Bazzano, he is married to Rina's sister, Maria. I nodded, saying, "He is willing to give me a job."

"Well then," they said, "we will release you."

What was the basis of you having to prove work when you had your own farm?

Oh, I wasn't allowed to go back to Smithfield.

Once they told me I could go and work for Bazzano, I asked them, "Why shouldn't I go back to my home?"

"Well, you can't, you can't go back to your property."

They told me to find lodging elsewhere, which I did. I found lodging with my wife in Pitt Street, Redfern. It was an okay little flat, with a gas stove on the veranda and a room with a bed in it and a bit of a table. That is where I took my wife with a child.

How did that feel to have to do that?

Well, you can just imagine. The problem was that I had my mother and two younger brothers in Smithfield in Woodpark Road.

Was your father interned as well?

Yes, my father was interned in Guildford. A group of buses came and took my father, my brother and took us to Liverpool. We were all interned together.

What brother is this?

Louie. Davino was interned before this, and he was in a town called Loveday.

Anyway, that was part of the story there. So, for me to go and see my mother and brother (from Redferm), I had to have a permit from the police. They gave me the permit, no problem, but I had to show the permit to the Smithfield police every time I went to see my mother and two brothers. When I returned in the evening, I had to go and to give the permit back. Sometimes it would be 9 or 10 o'clock at night. Often, I visited the station and would go back again to my family. I got to know the sergeant at Redfern Police Station, and he was a very nice gentleman.

What was his name?

I don't remember his name.

What month was this?

Possibly May, no, June. I was interned for two months, so when I went to Redfern it was two months after. From Liverpool, they transferred us to Cowra; I was also interned in Cowra.

In Cowra, the Japanese were also interned. Italian soldiers, as well! There were about fifty metres of barbed wire between the other camps and us. They allowed us one newspaper a week and we would all get together in one of the halls, at night. When we got the paper, we had a fellow that would read the paper and give us the news of how Britain was going. It was *The Herald*. The newspaper recounted a detailed version of how the war was going, what was happening, and one thing or the other. This fellow used to read the articles that were printed. We all stayed there after dinner to listen to it.

One day, that same fellow came up with a beauty.

He said he was from Queensland. "You know what? My wife wrote to me. She wrote to me to tell me that there is a terrible drought, that everything is so dry, there is not a blade of grass anywhere. She cannot even grow a patch of *radicchio* because there is no water, and the ground is so hard that she cannot manage!"

This fellow had a bright idea. Knowing that all the communication was censored, he wrote to this wife and said, "Dear wife, what has come over you? What are you thinking? Digging up the garden! You know what we have buried there! You leave things alone."

So, the wife writes back: "Oh, I got the scare of my life! Here comes a truck full of soldiers, with picks and shovels and they dig the whole garden up! Looking for what we are supposed to have hidden there!"

Then, this same mischievous fellow replies to his wife, "Now you can plant your potato and *radicchio*!"

Can you just imagine all of their bloomin' faces?!

That poor wife!

At that point, when a man is reading you the newspaper written by the Allies, how did it portray the enemy ... you guys?

Oh well, we had to take what was said.

What was said?

The Allies advancing here, bombing there. Germany getting Poland and all this business. Then, going to the Russian front and all of this. We didn't know what to think or what to do.

Did you hear any news about Italy?

No.

How did you feel about Australia, at that point? Were you bitter?

No, I wasn't bitter about Australia. I could not be bitter against Australia. The only thing that I resented was that I had so many friends that I played football with, and they were called into the army, and I wasn't! At that stage, I wasn't naturalised. The strange things that amazed me, and everyone else to a certain extent, was that we had fathers interned with us that had their sons in the army!

So, Italian men whose sons were born in Australia, were fighting against Italy and Germany?

Yes, that is true. That is the thing we thought, *How come?*

How did those men feel?

You can just imagine how the poor fathers felt. They were crying.

How old were you and your father when you were interned?

My father was between fifty-nine and sixty-one. I was married at twenty-eight and I turned twenty-nine in jail.

I was only in Cowra for one month. I was only interned for two months and then I was released.

Did you have any correspondence with Nanna then?

Yes, Rina and I wrote to each other.

Back in Redfern, I befriended this sergeant at the police station. He got curious, this fellow, and he said, "How come you need a permit to go and see your mother?" I told him the story about being interned and how they wouldn't let me go and live in my home, and I didn't know why.

"How come?" he asked. "You own the place."

"Yes," I said. "I've owned the place for many years, since 1932! I can't understand it."

"Oh. Let me have a look at your file and see if there is any reason why you shouldn't go back to your house."

A couple of weeks went past, and I met up with him again. He advised, "There is nothing in your file that incriminates you, but it says you can't go and live in your own place."

At this stage, I knew what the officer in Smithfield had said about buying the property and, of course, he got very nasty himself.

The Redfern Sergeant said, "You go back, no one can do anything to you."

"Under the circumstances," I replied, "I don't want to. I have a young mother here with a child. How can I compromise their living, their lives, by doing this? I couldn't do it!"

Some more time went past. Then, the sergeant in Redfern approached me saying, "There is a Captain Davis in Castlereagh Street. He has an office there and he is the Director of Enemy Aliens. Go and see him!"

"I will," I said. So off I went to see Captain Davis.

I was working with Bazzano in a factory at Newtown doing the machinery and customising aluminium for aircraft. I was concentrating on aluminium produce, making the parts, and then they had to be machined. That is what I had to do. Together with Leo, I had to do the customs and then they had to be machined, and I used to do the machining and complete the job.

I went to see Captain Davis. Once there, he said, "Come in, sit down." He called a fellow and said, "Go and get me the file on Mr Zadro."

As he looked through my file, I watched as his expression changed. He looked really concerned and serious. He said to me, "The policeman in Smithfield is so and so."

"Yes", I said.

"He is a friend of mine," he said. "You can't go back to your place in Smithfield."

"But sir, why?"

"I told you; you can't go back."

I was getting really angry and in a loud voice I stated, "Tell me why I can't go to Smithfield, please; I want a reason!"

He yelled. "I told you; you can't go to Smithfield. Now get out of here! Before I intern you again!"

I said, "If you have any reason, you do that!"

"Get out!" he screamed.

That was that.

I reported this to the sergeant in Redfern. "Ah," he said. "What is this world coming to?"

Time went by and one day I came across him again and he advised, "Look, Captain Davis has been demoted. He is not in the job anymore. Now, there is Captain so-and-so (I forget his name); go and see him and see if you get a better result."

How long after was that?

It was four or five weeks later when I went and saw this other gentleman. Regretfully, I don't remember his name. I don't know if it was Roger or something like that. He called me in, and he went and got my file. When he looked at it, he looked up at me and declared, "Of course you can go back to your home. What have you been doing in Redfern?"

"Thank you, and thank God, to be able to go back to my home."

He gave me a permit, and I met up with the sergeant at Redfern again, as he wanted to know the results.

"I told you," he said. "You could have gone back anytime you wanted to! Don't you mind about Captain Davis."

By then, he knew what the Smithfield Police wanted to do. They wanted to get possession of our home: five acres and our home at Smithfield because it was right in the town, in Oxford Street.

So, because of that corrupt policeman in Smithfield, you weren't allowed to go home all that time?

Yes, all that time, we were not allowed to go back. Anyway, finally, we went back to Smithfield, and we were back in our own house.

One day, as I was walking about the town doing some shopping, this same (corrupt) policeman came up to me. "What are you doing here? Where is your permit?"

"I don't need one! Thank you," I replied.

That was the policeman, the one that I had to show the permit. He was shocked that I was back in Smithfield. He didn't expect me. He said, "Where is your permit?"

"I didn't need one. I don't need one!" I replied. "I am back in my place!"

And that was it.

What happened to that policeman from Smithfield?

Well, after a time, he got demoted from his position. It wasn't my doing. I think it was something to do with corruption. That is why he was demoted, someone reported him. Unfortunately, after some years, he was reinstated back into the police force.

When you went back to your house, what was it like?

It was like a dream. Actually, I should ask Rina what she felt. For me, it was like a dream. I had a head like this ... (gestures a dreamy head) ... but the war was still going on and I still felt like I was an enemy alien.

Then, the government asked for volunteers to grow vegetables for the army, so I volunteered.

Why?

Because I felt that I owed the country something, that I wanted to do something for Australia.

I don't think that anybody would think that I pretended to be anything that I am not. I have always said one thing: I feel very strongly about this — it takes a good Italian to be a very good Australian.

If you are a bad Italian, you can't be a good Australian. You can't be anything. If you regret your own country, deny your own heritage, your own parents, well, what are you? That is why I have always kept this line and used it publicly.

Life went on, and eventually, the war ended, and things got back to normal.

Everyone used to go about their business. Like I said, I was growing vegetables for the government.

And then your family grew?

Yes it did! By this time, we had another boy, Arthur[17].

So, the rains came again?

Yes, I was able to pump the water from the creek and I used to grow a lot of cabbage and cauliflower. That was my contract. The army used to come and pick the stuff up and count it. They mainly wanted cabbage. They used to pay us so much.

What percentage of your garden did you give to the army?

All of garden was used for crops for the army, all of what I used to produce.

So, you didn't go to the markets at that stage?

No, I didn't go back to the markets every day. But what they didn't want I used to take to the markets. One day, I went to the markets and met up with Frank Vassallo.[18] He came in his military uniform; he had come to say goodbye to me. He told me that he was joining the army, and he was going overseas. Of course, you can imagine how we felt, we embraced one another.

Was Frank a good friend of yours?

Oh yes.

---

[17] Arthur was named Arturo at birth. He was born in 1943.
[18] Amy Vassallo's brother.

How did you become friends with him?

We used to mix socially because I knew his sisters, Amy, and all of them. We used to run church functions together.

And Frank went to join the Australian army?

Yes, Frank joined the army. Bill, his brother, is still about though. We met him a little while ago at the doctors with his wife; in fact, two weeks ago. We had a lot to say to each other.

I was saying goodbye to Frank, and as I wished him good luck, there was a fellow standing away, at the side, looking at us. I didn't take any notice of him. Frank went, and this fellow came over and he said, "What did you talk about with that soldier? What do you have to do with him?"

I felt very embarrassed; you have no idea. I told him that he was a friend of mine and that he got called up and was going to join the army and that I was not called up.

He walked away.

Was that guy who questioned you Italian?

No, he was Australian. I had never seen him before. Spies, you know, they used to do that. They used to keep an eye on the enemy aliens. They should have kept an eye on their own, never mind us. I know some stories of desertion and things like that, all these things were going on.

How did the whole experience of being interned by a government, that you had lived under faithfully and loyally for fifteen years, make you feel?

Oh, you can just imagine. I was really, really dejected. I thought, *But why?*

I asked my father, who was a returned soldier from the First World War—he had been decorated—and I said, "How come? What for?"

My father never once said anything against Australia.

It seems so ironic, the whole story you just told, where you go and get told you had to register at Merrylands with people that you knew. Then you're interned, and then you decide to grow vegetables for the Australian soldiers. It is a wild tale Nonno.

I only knew the policeman. The other authorities, they were all strangers. The ones that came and picked me up in Merrylands, at the depot, I had never seen them before. In fact, when we were conscripted, more or less for the Labour Corps, you had to go for a medical examination. I went for the medical examination, and I was declared fit. Next thing, I don't know whether it was the same day or the same week, I was coming back from Merrylands with the bike when they came and picked me up. They didn't want me in the Labour Corps anymore.

So, there was a difference? At one point you were going in the Labour Corps, and one point you were going to be interned?

Yeah, that is why they visited us—my brother Louie and me. He had to go to the Labour Corps, as he was conscripted. He had not much notice, and Davino was the same. They only had notice to get themselves a cup, toothbrush, little shaving things, and clothes. They had to get ready because they were going to be picked up. Davino finished up in the town of Neilrex making charcoal.[19]

---

[19] In North-Western New South Wales.

How long was Davino there for?

He was there for the duration of the war. But before that he was interned! The reason was because he had come to Australia in 1939, just before the war broke out. And they suspected him more than those of us who had been here longer.

What was your life like after internment?

In 1939, I was very active with the Smithfield church. In the beginning, Father Collins from Liverpool used to come once a month and give mass in Smithfield, in the St Gertrude Church, which is still there. Then bit by bit, he couldn't come anymore, and they used to take it in turns. Two Benedictine priests took turns and came every Sunday.

Finally, Smithfield was given to the Benedictine priests. They came from America. The first priest was Fr Cornelus. They started to get around to meet the people. They were organising the church and tried to get the schools going.

I knew a lot of the Italians from Bossley Park and I knew that they were very fond of singing and playing *Bocce*. So much so, that one fellow by the name of Seb Crestani, who lived up in Horsley Park and who had a lot of friends, used to have people go up to his place. He made a *Bocce* court, and they started to play *Bocce*. They used to get quite a lot of people. Of course, with playing *Bocce* out in the sun, they used to get thirsty. So, what happened was the losers had to pay for drinks for the winners. He had to provide the beer for them and, by doing so, he had to pay for it. Someone was jealous and reported him and the police confiscated all his beer.

A little while later there was a wedding in Smithfield – of Primo Finato and Clara Pezzoto, and I was invited to the wedding. There was this Crestani, complaining about the police confiscating his beer. "Well," I said, "why don't we build a club and have the selling of liquor made legal?"

"Oh," a fellow chimed in, "who can get enough Italians together to build a club?"

"Well, if we don't try, we won't know, will we? It's an idea. Why not try it?"

We got together, and we formed a committee. We thought about approaching the Italian community to see what response we would get by asking them to contribute fifty pounds each.

Who was on the committee?

I was in, and there was Provino Sartor, Ruben Sarto, Lorenzo Zamprogno, and Sebastiano Crestani. Then, we involved Oscar Michelini – he was our first president. There was Benedetti, Andres Zueliani, and Peter Sebastani. Anyway, there were about fourteen or fifteen of us. At the first meeting, we were the first ones to contribute fifty pounds each so that we could lead by example and then ask the Italian community to also do so.

How much money did you get?

Well, I think we raised about 4,000 pounds. The Club President was Oscar Michelini, and his assistant was Eustacchio Del Bin, as the Club Secretary. He used to keep the books for Michelini, and he also used to prepare correspondence. Anyway, we then decided to look around for a place. The Sartors had bought the land, that Club Marconi is now on in Bossley Park, for about 4,000 and something pounds. They eventually sold it to the Club for the same price they got it.

After that, we got together; we had to get someone to draw up a constitution. Three of our committee members went to a Catholic Club in Griffith to see what kind of constitution they had. They came back with a constitution and, of course, we had a solicitor examine the constitution and we had to make some alterations to suit our area.

What ideals is the club built on?

The Club was formed to give the Italian community a sense of togetherness. In those early years, the newcomers had to do all the work, and they were very, very homesick. They had a lot of nostalgia to cope with and of course, having an establishment like Club Marconi would provide a place for them to meet and enjoy themselves, express their opinions, talk about their country, their families and get together in an atmosphere of joy.

We had people participating in sports, *Bocce* in particular, that is what we started with. In the youth centre there was soccer, which I promoted. I was to become the Director of Soccer of Club Marconi.

The response of the community towards the betterment of the Club was fantastic and, of course, it was very encouraging. There was a lot of support for the committee to go on and really apply themselves to the highest of possibilities, in order to better the Club and give more amenities to the community. This was the basis on which we formed our constitution.

When the Club was formed it wasn't a political setup. It was nothing to do with politics, it was just to quench the thirst that developed from leaving your own country and living in a strange one.

The Club allowed people to come together and be able to express and describe their weekend, how they worked, how they prospered, what they encountered, their episodes, their families and children at school. Living in a country without the knowledge of the language and not understanding was the hardest. But our children, they flourished with their English, flourished with their studies, and they began to win trophies. They participated in all these Australian sports and therefore we, the Italian community, became integrated into the community. That is what I, myself in particular, wanted. I wanted things to be involved in; I wanted to be in the system, and I was. I am very happy to have experienced that within the Italian community.

The children of our members, they really responded to the activities of our schools.

But is it just a club for Italians?

No. The Club was not restricted to Italians; it was open to all comers. When I became president, I advocated to address the community needs at different occasions of reunions, festivities, dances and so on.

You mean the Fairfield Community?

It was not just the Fairfield community, even larger. Any chance I got, I promoted the Italian community to the wider society.

I have always said I emphasised the fact that we chose the name Marconi because of his genius, because of what he had achieved, with television and communications[20]. I reflected on our efforts in this way. We chose the name Marconi because he embraced the whole world with his genius. It is that world we must embrace, the whole Italian community and the Australian community.

Club Marconi embraced everybody. I advocated for myself in that way not so long ago at a Club dinner. Recently (1999), we had the presidents of the Chambers of Commerce from all over the world visit with us. The Italian Chamber of Commerce came to Sydney with the President of the Chamber of Commerce in Sydney, Mr Nick Scali (the furniture man). He is an old acquaintance of mine that I have not seen for many years. At one stage, he was President of APIA when I was President of Club Marconi and I advocated to meet him.[21] At this reunion, I was introduced to the President of the Italian Chamber of Commerce.

I was invited to this dinner, and I sat there with several other old club members who were also invited. We sat together with the bank manager, the one that balances Club Marconi with all its projects. I must say that Club Marconi holds the bank in high esteem because they advanced millions to the Club for expenses. So much so, that I jokingly asked the manager: "Does Marconi pay interest on the millions they owe to the bank?"

With a smile, he quickly responded, "Oh yes!"

---

[20] Guglielmo Giovanni Maria Marconi, First Marquis of Marconi FRSA (25 April 1874- 20 July 1937) was an Italian inventor and electrical engineer, known for his creation of a practical radio wave-based wireless telegraph system. Marconi was credited as the inventor of radio, and he shared the 1909 Nobel Prize in Physics with Karl Ferdinand Braun.
[21] APIA stands for *Associazione Polisportiva Italo-Australiana*. It was a very popular Italian sporting and social club in Lilyfield, founded in 1954.

Mr Labozzetta, the president of the day, then came around to say hello to everybody. He shook hands with everyone and a fellow there got me to tell him what I asked the bank manager. Mr Labozetta said, "There you are! There is a member who still has got the Club at heart."

I had the occasion to meet a lot of old acquaintances that night; they were people I haven't seen for a long time. Because of my age, I don't frequent the Club as often as I'd like to or participate in the activities of the Club any longer. Nevertheless, I still have the Club at heart. I consider it one of my big families.

What do you believe was and is your personal contribution to the building of Club Marconi?

I insisted that we should have a Youth Centre. Do you recollect that? I *insisted* that we should have a Youth Centre. Knowing the nature of the Italians and their attachment to families, they would not come to the Club and leave their children at home. They had to have their children with them, so I thought if we don't find accommodation for the children, we won't be able to help the parents. This was brought about because of the liquor laws that youth under the age of twenty-one could not go to any club. They had to have a special building for themselves, so this is what we created. At one stage there we had 250 members and, of course, when it was established, the President told me, "Zadro, you wanted the Youth Centre, so there it is. Now, you look after it."

I considered it my baby.

Who said this to you?

The President said it in a committee meeting.

Who was the President then?

The President, at the time, was Vic Fiorelli. He was the second president. He turned out to be a very good friend of mine and we really worked well together; collaborated really well. Eventually we got to the stage where we felt that the Club needed extending because of the participation of the citizens of the district. Not only were there Italians but other nationalities; Australians and everybody. Through soccer, we managed to have Australian players. We had a mix of interest because the club began to be considered as a very popular venue for recreation.

Did the soccer come out of the Youth Centre?

Yes, it was I who created the soccer club from the Youth Centre.

And when did this happen?

Well, that's very important. I'd like to be accurate with this because it was before I became president and that happened in 1960. I would say, with confidence, that it might have been a little before. Late in 1959.

So, let's go back a bit because we're jumping everywhere. You said to the committee, "Look, we need a Youth Centre, and I think these are the reasons we need a Youth Centre." You explained that, and the President replied, "There's your room, there's your Youth Centre!" What did you do with it?

We notified the parents of the Youth Centre about our idea to have a soccer program, and we found there was a terrific response. People used to come to the Club and take the youth to the Youth Centre, which we called the Christina

Room.[22] That was the Youth Centre Hall. I was responsible for the first activities, the gatherings and keeping of records, names, who they were, and the families who participated in one thing and the other.

It wasn't very long before I found there was a necessity to form my own committee for the Youth Centre, so they could run themselves and come to me with their ideas they wanted to promote. The families were not only very responsive to the soccer, but they also created a *filma dramatico* — a play. We organised a group, and they started to perform.

Which is still going today?

Well, today it's not that type of thing that is considered, what's more popular now are the physical sports like soccer, bowls, and tennis.

So out of this committee, the soccer club started?

Yes. The soccer team was created and started off. There were objections because of the cost involved with soccer and whether the Club could cope with the extra expenses. We proved the cost was minimal and worthwhile because it used to attract a lot of people to the Club. I had to prove this to the president, of the time, because he was really worried, as were many others. However, I convinced him that we wouldn't be too extravagant with anything, we would just take things as they came and progress as the finances permitted.

That was done, and we managed to progress all the time. We used to play for the competition, at the time, which was made up of the local group of soccer teams in the area. We were competing with other clubs in order to get into the

---

[22] Christina was the name of Marconi's daughter.

competition and we ended up being finalists. We had to beat Smithfield, Guildford, Fairfield, and then, we had to beat Manly.

Manly was on top of the list. Either they won the tournament, or we did. I was there when we played at Manly with our players. I got them in the dressing room before the match. I encouraged them to put one hand on top of the other and I said, "Promise that you're all for one and one for all."

They yelled out, "Yes, one for all and all for one!"

The game was a terrific game, very well fought, and Marconi managed to score the only goal, so we got into the Federation.

How old were the boys?

Oh, in those days, the boys ranged from fifteen to eighteen.

From there on, did the soccer become an entity of its own?

No. At that time, the soccer was still at Club Marconi, but then we reached the stage where the demand was huge. However, I lost the administration with soccer because I became Club President, so it meant someone else took over. Under the new direction, there were some very ambitious people. They wanted to buy players, and they wanted to do so many things; I contested this move.

The Youth Club President asked me for $15,000, as well as more money, to fix up the soccer field. I showed him that we couldn't afford it, and we had to take things steady and consider all sports to keep everything alive. He didn't agree with me. He said if I wanted to be president for the rest of my life, I had to do this.

I told him to go to hell — he and his committee! It was close to the election, you see, and he was trying to bribe me. He started up propaganda that I was against soccer, even though, I had started it! I lost the election that year. There was another man elected president, that was Spiga. I was happy that the following year, at the elections, I was re-elected.

How did it feel to lose the election?

You can just imagine. I was really disgusted, really frustrated. I often wondered, *how come people are blind? What are they doing?*

How long were you in for the first time?

I was president for two years, and then the second time, three years.[23]

Now we have covered the aims and the purposes of forming the Club. Now let's look at the extension of the Club, if you like. Two years later, in 1960, we were already financial enough to approach the bank and ask for a loan to extend the Club.

How much was the loan?

I forget what the figure was exactly. We borrowed from the bank, but it could have been something like $300,000. Mr Arena, an architect, drew up the plans for us. He was the husband of Mrs Arena, the politician, Franca Arena. I know them personally, both of them. We found his designs showed the plans of the building was too high in the air and looked funny. We were thinking all the time, what could be done? You see, where the original club was built, the ground was sloping. So, I said to the committee,

---

[23] 1966-1969 and 1971-1973.

"I think I've got a solution. Instead of going up so much, we can cut at least a couple of metres down, by building a split-level."

They laughed at me. They didn't think it was nice, but I was so convinced that I kept repeating it at every meeting we had, so much so that the President got fed up with my insistence. Finally, he stated, "Look, we will call the architect to one of our meetings and you tell him. Propose to him what you're thinking we should do."

Fair enough, I thought.

The architect came to one meeting, and the President said, "Zadro here has got an idea and it's to have a split-level." And the architect spread his hands and nodded, "Why didn't I think of it?!"

So, the idea was implemented. The architect said it was the right thing to do, stating that it was a very modern trend.

When the idea for the Club for the Finato wedding was discussed, which led to asking people to contribute fifty pounds, what were your personal aspirations for the Club? What did *you* want Club Marconi to be? Back then, right at the beginning before it even started?

My vision was for the Italian community to establish itself as a cultural and civilised people in the community and to partake in the activities of the community. So much so that we befriended the Smithfield RSL, Blacktown Workers Club, Cabramatta RSL, and the Cabra-Vale Diggers Club, as they used to call it.

Every function we had at our club; we invited their presidents. It was very regular, and they used to do the same.

That's what I wanted for the Club. I wanted the Italian community to be a part of the community, the Australian Community—part and parcel. Also, to show that we were capable of doing something concrete, something worthwhile.

To prove, in a way, that Italians are beneficial to the Australian community?

Well, in a sense, indirectly. I would say that being constructive and participating in the Italian activities, whether they be sport, buildings, projects, or anything like that. In essence, the Italians would honour themselves and would portray an image of themselves that they could be appreciated and recognised as worthy, and worthy to be Australians.

How important was that in the post-World War Two era? To build that positive identity of Italians in Australia, as *Italian-Australians* after a war, where the Allies fought the fascists?

We built the Club after the war. I'm afraid we had an extra mission to really justify ourselves. To really show that we were a civilised people and that we have our own culture. That we were willing to participate in the Australian culture, the Australian way of life. I think we succeeded in doing that very efficiently and it made me very, very happy. I still am happy that our community is recognised and respected for its work and its worth.

How would you describe the character of Italians in the eyes of Australians today? How do you feel Italians are portrayed more generally in the community?

When I landed in Australia and the years before the war, as far as the Italian community is concerned, they were considered, at least this was my impression, as an inferior people despite their culture and history.

So much so, that in some textbooks and primary school, the ones that Chana and Terry—my brothers—were reading for their schoolwork, it said Italy entered the war in 1918. My father was conscripted in 1915 with all his brothers, and I was wondering why that was in the books my brothers were reading. I felt uneasy about that kind of thing. People in Australia were not learning the truth of what we had experienced.

Italians (and other foreigners) were not tolerated to speak their own language in public. If they were in a shop, hotel, or anywhere and they spoke their own language, there was always somebody who resented it. People would turn around and say in a rude tone, "Why don't you speak English, you dagos?"

You see, that's what the phrase used to be, and I used to detest it; I killed myself about it. It made me very emotional. I told my wife that what we needed was to really get amongst them, and with them, to try and show them who we really were.

CHAPTER FIVE
Inspiring a Legacy

"Not participating and not doing is the easy way out of everything. It is important to participate in the things that really matter."

How did you felt when you became president in terms of the 'success' of your migration? Was becoming President of Club Marconi, an important signifier of your success and your personal contribution to the community?

Now, I would like to tell you this much before we go any further. Before the Club was established, I was involved in St Gertrude's Catholic Church in Smithfield. I had a committee there that built the church and the schools.

We used the first hall that we built as a church and a fundraising amenity, for dances and things like that. I remember, one year, the committee raised 5,000 pounds in one function. That was a lot of money then. We never had a permanent fixture in Smithfield. There used to be a priest that used to come from Sydney who used to say mass at Smithfield, but before that, Smithfield was under the Liverpool Parish. The Liverpool priest used to come once a month to say mass in the old hall.

Then, under the Benedictine priests, Smithfield was declared a parish through the hierarchy unto itself. The parish was given to the Benedictine Fathers.

The first Benedictine Father was from Ceylon, India. The poor fellow came here, and he didn't have a home. He didn't have an address to go to. He managed to borrow a push bike, and he used to go around and visit the Italian community. He would go to one family, and they would say, "There is another one over there," and so on.

This happened so often that, one day, he got his trouser leg caught in his chain and he ripped his trousers. Somebody told him about us in Smithfield and he come around and Rina fixed his trousers up. He sat on a chair with his legs straight out in front of him, and Rina fixed it up for him. He was such a nice person. This was Father Farina. When he was transferred, our whole community gave him a farewell party, and everyone spoke very highly of him.

The American Church Fathers came here after Farina. They were very young and very full of zeal and wanted to get on and do things. They got the Italian community to participate. They emphasised the need for schools and the Italian community responded very, very well. I formed a committee to raise funds and, like I said, we constructed the first hall. We presented one of the fathers with 5,000 pounds. And who do you think came to inaugurate this hall? Cardinal Gilroy. In fact, he spent a lot of time with me in the group.

What was Cardinal Gilroy like?

Oh, Cardinal Gilroy was a beautiful person; he was a real gentleman. He used to love the Italians, and he spoke Italian, as well. At this time, we had the CYO (Catholic Youth Organisation). I used to get my sons and daughters to belong to this association. Sometimes, I used to get them all on my three-tonne truck and take them out to picnics and parties; kicking a ball, out in the country, next to a river, wherever it might be, climbing or doing something of that nature.

Was the Catholic Youth Organisation (CYO) a big organisation then?

The CYO was well organised in those days. After that, I became involved with the Club, as I told you. I resigned from that committee, and I started with Club Marconi after the discussion we had at the Finato's wedding. Then, the Benedictine Fathers started saying mass at Bossley Park. There was only a little church there; it was only a wooden structure. We used to have Father Romano saying mass there every Sunday, but it was taken from the Benedictine Fathers because they could not administer that church.

Anyway, it became a parish on its own. It became the Bossley Park Parish and was given to the diocesan priests; that is how it remains now. After a while, we built the new chapel with Peter Neville, the first parish priest.

I remember him coming to me in his first days of the parish. He asked for my opinion of the schools in the area and about building a Catholic school.

I was frank when I answered him: "If you want to have success, you must have a Catholic School, because [that's how] you catch and grow a parish."

The decision was made to construct the school, and they named it Mary Immaculate Primary School. There are about 300 children attending that school now.

With the church committee that I was involved in we set about raising money for the Bossley Park parish and we contributed around $30,000. That mainly came from the Italian community. We donated many things, such as the crucifix, the organ, the fridge, and lots of other things. There was a multitude of things that we worked towards.

When I asked you, how did you feel when you became president and how that reflects on your whole experience in Australia, you went to your experiences at Smithfield. Did that feel the same for you in some respects? When you started your committee at Smithfield, was that a moment for you when you stood back and thought, my life has been good here?

I never praised myself for anything. My personal feelings were that I was so happy. Nights like the function, that I mentioned before, where we couldn't fit the people in the bloomin' hall, made me so happy. That night we invited the Italian Consul, and we only offered him a cup of tea. He came with his followers, you know, his secretary and his vice-consul. I remember seeing him looking at all the people.

He said, "Zadro, how did you manage to get all these Italians together? You know, in Sydney, we are lucky if we get 40-50 and we can't get any more to participate. Look at this crowd; this is fantastic. My congratulations!"

It really impressed him that so many Italians in the area answered the call to come and contribute. The Consulate was happy to see people get together, to meet each other, and to discuss things that we needed to talk about (as a community). Such topics included the nostalgic feelings of home. It was important to talk to people that had the same feelings and thoughts. It was very important for migrants to do this.

This was because, as Italians, we had to fight to get ourselves understood. We had to fight for so many things. Although the laws of the country were really good for everybody, we had to contend with people that didn't always think of us in a good light, and personally, I understood that. We were entering and infringing on something that was 'theirs'. This was during the Depression, and we had to live and work in the community. We had to strive so much.

The Italian community around here came because of the Depression. It was a hard time for everyone. We strived together, though. There was no work, so we had to do something. Sometimes, one person rented some land and started to grow vegetables. In order to do that, he had to have help, and in this way, people would get their lives together.

In the Smithfield Church, I knew so many young fellows that thought the way I did. I started to build some respect in the church, and we would all work together to carry out an idea.

In 1939, we got Davino, my brother, to come over here, just before the war broke out. He came with my cousin, John, to Australia. Davino had been in college for so many years. He acquired a terrific knowledge of music, and he was able to play an organ. He also had a beautiful voice. He had the ability to instruct a choir, so I got a group of men together and we formed a choir.

The choir was formed for our church; for hymns to sing at mass and vespas and things like that. Oh, Davino had a fantastic voice! The choir was great; he ended up having about forty-five members, both male and female.

And Davino was the conductor?

Davino was the conductor, the one that provided the music, the one that conducted the rehearsal. We were invited to go and sing at the mass in St Mary's Cathedral.

I would like to go back to the Club ... what did being the President of the Club mean to you?

Firstly, I was asked to apply to be the president, and I refused. Then when they insisted that I apply for the position, I did. Although I had experience in committees and running meetings and things of that nature, it was a new experience for me.

I was determined that I had to get voted in, and I thought to myself, *I have to do my utmost now to do the right thing for the members*. Being a little bit impatient, and in a hurry to do things, sometimes I used to get the backs up of the committee, because of my insistence to do things differently.

Like what?

When committee discussions about certain things at the Club took place, like certain improvements, I found a lot of diddling about and lots of arguments. I used to get impatient. For instance, one year, we had a terrible, hot summer, and we didn't have any air-conditioning at the Club. It was so hot that nobody would come to the Club; they would go to the beaches and things like that, but they wouldn't come to the Club because it was like an oven!

We used to have a monthly meeting, and at one of these meetings, I proposed to the committee that we had to get some fans in the Club, and do something, otherwise we wouldn't get anybody in. A few said alright that it was a good idea. It was decided that I had to get some quotes.

After this meeting, the temperatures soared, and so, I got hold of the Secretary Manager, and I said, "Let's just go and get the fans."

I think we bought five of these fans on a stand at fifteen pounds each. I put them in the Club, and people started to come to the Club again, and sit around them.

When we had the next meeting, I was criticised because I went and bought the fans without the approval of the full committee.

I told the committee: "Look, the next meeting wasn't for another three weeks, and you know what the weather has been like. I found that it was an essential thing to do. If anything, I expected you to approve what I have done and say thanks. Okay, you are right, I should have waited for you, but I thought I would do the right thing by the Club, and the members obviously appreciate it and that is more important."

Anyway, that was that.

When you were the President, how much time did you spend at the Club?

Oh, I used to be there very often, at least three or four times a week, sometimes every day. Three or four times a week, in the evenings, and every weekend. Sometimes there were things going on at the Club that I didn't like, and I wanted to keep an eye on things.

For instance, there were a couple of detectives that used to come and have dinner every Sunday at Club Marconi. These detectives did this for quite a few months. I got to know about it, so I went up there Sunday midday and I saw these two fellows come in. They signed the book, and they went into the dining room.

I went to the doorman, and I asked, "Listen, those two fellows, who are they?"

He replied, "They are detectives."

"They are coming here for dinner, I believe?"

"Oh, yes."

"You have to look after people like that. You never know when you are going to need them."

I was furious. I said, "WHAT! Look after those people because you may need them! The Club is run according to the law, and we don't need anybody!"

I shook my head, saying, "So, this time you pay for the dinner of the two men, understand?"

He went and told the Secretary Manager. The Secretary Manager came over to me and said, "Zadro, isn't making the doorman pay for the dinner a bit drastic?"

"No, not at all."

"But you insist that he should pay for them."

"I tell you what we do. I want him to pay for the dinner, and then we will repay him the money."

"Alright, we will do that," the Secretary Manager agreed.

In another incident, the Club Manager said to me, "Committee Member so-and-so has some visitors here, and he entertained them with dinner. He came and asked me for fifty dollars to pay for their dinner. I gave him the fifty dollars, and he put in into his pocket and then he signed the book for entertainment." (He put the dinner on the Club expenses account.)

"Oh, I see, this is what is going on," I said.

A while later, the same man went broke with his firm. He came to the Club, and he had a cheque for $250 to cash. The

Bar Manager came over to me: "Look, so and so, gave me this cheque to cash. What should I do?"

"No, don't cash it," I said. So, he went back and told him.

"The President said not to cash it so I can't cash it for you." There was a more senior staff working behind the bar, at this time. He heard what was going on and he gave the staff member that asked me the sack, then and there. It was a big mess, and we sorted it all out and the man got his job back, but this is the type of behaviour I wanted to keep an eye on.

When you are watching the TV and you see the soccer, Marconi versus someone, what do you feel?

I want Marconi to win, and if they don't win, I feel that I have to have a reason. For instance, this year's misfortunes with sick players and everything, they weren't doing very well at all, losing every game against people inferior to them.

I thought, *Gee Whizz, we have a very well-known coach, a very capable person, notable who had won last year's competition in Queensland, what is the reason? The players are fantastic, the Club paid a lot of money for them, why don't they give of themselves?*

How do you feel when Club Marconi receives negative media coverage? How do you react to it?

We went through a tough period over these last couple of years. This involved the sale of a player with money missing here and money missing there. It hurt me very, very much.

When I see Club Marconi negatively talked about in the press, I think they are talking about the prestige of the Italian community, because we are a symbol of the Italian community. For example, last week a fellow shot another man in the car park. I think to myself, *why does this type of thing have to happen here at the Club*? I was really upset by the whole affair.

You personally feel hurt by that?

Yes, I do, I do. I feel why come to Club Marconi to do things like that? Club Marconi should be considered a home for everybody without cultural distinction. That is the fundamental reason we built the club and called it Club Marconi. Because of Marconi's ideals, his principles, and his values, and everything like that.

To see this type of incident hurts me very much. I met a fellow down at the Club, and he happened to be from the same region as the man that did the shooting. He asked me how I felt. "Oh," I said, "I am very sorry. I felt better before last Wednesday."

"Yes," he nodded, "you are right."

He understood what I meant. Incidents like this harm everyone (and the Club's reputation).

If people do these types of things, you dishonour your own kind. I believe that we need to be praised as a community; we need to have a community that is worthy of Australia. I have said it repetitively, "It takes a very good Italian to become a good Australian." A bad Italian will never be a good Australian, or anything else. This is an observation of my experience of seventy years in Australia.

If an honest working Italian, a cultured person in the Italian language, and Italian way of life, comes to Australia and becomes a good Australian, he will be accepted. I have proof of that.

This belief has stayed with me. At the Club, I insisted on having both flags raised — the Australian and the Italian. Now if you asked me who would I put allegiance to or for whom I would fight, my answer would be, I would like to be neutral. But if I were really pressed, I would have to accept Australia. My family, they are Australians born and bred, so I have to accept Australia.

You are eight-six years old. What role in the Club Marconi community do you have now?

Now, due to my age, and my declining health, I am not participating in too many activities. However, the Club recognised my contributions, and they made me a life member. That gave me a ticket with which I can go anywhere and participate in anything in the Club. In fact, they gave me a sticker with a membership that won't expire until the year 3000!

Do you think your presence at Club Marconi is still appreciated, still valued, and respected?

Yes, very much. I am surprised when, every time I go to the Club, if I am at a table for dinner, people come up to me and say, "Very pleased to meet you. How are you?" Dozens of people come up and say: "Lovely to see you. Can I buy you a drink? Can I do this? Can I do that?"

Would it be fair to say that one role that you play in the Club now is as a reminder of the origins of the Club?

I think I am a reminder. When people come up to me from around the Club, some say that I am a bastion of the Club. Oh, very good! What can I say? I have badge number 08 and I can't get away from that. There are only three of us left from the original committee alive.

What do you believe are the steps that the Club can take to maintain its sense of origin and history as it moves into the next millennium?

That is a very good question, and I will answer it this way. I do appreciate and I am aware of the necessity for expansion, the population around us in our community and the increased number of members of the Club (over 20,000) it does warrant expansion.

However, I believe that you can expand too much; you can go over the top in spending. Every community that frequents Club Marconi, has also progressed, often having their own associations. One of these days, we will find that there are clubs springing up from all these nationalities. For example, the Spanish, the Greeks, and Lebanese. Of course, that will decrease the number of attendances at the Club. I would feel that perhaps that shifting of the community makeup should be looked into very thoroughly and we shouldn't expand beyond a certain limit.

At present, the Club is in a fantastic financial position, but that is all due to a lot of the poker machines — gambling! The present administration seemed to create more facilities for gambling. I am conscious of what gambling does to a married man, and a single man who will get married one day, create a family, buy a home, and things like that. Gambling is not a healthy influence on this.

When I think of all the expansion plans, I want to ask, what is it all for? Who is it for? The personal glory of some, or is it a necessity to the community? Are we doing this for the community? Where does the Italian community come into it?

If you want to honour yourself, the Club, and the Italian community, there are many ways of doing it. There are members that have sick families; why don't we look after them? We have parents that have children who are very capable and could do well at studies, but don't have the finance; why don't we try to find out and do something for them? Don't just do it for the Italian community, do it for the local community.

This is how I see it. To get others to see it in the same way is a different thing.

The present administration is losing the values in which we erected the Club. It is losing them very rapidly. They are only concerned about the money and what they can do with it. They want the Club to be big. So, they in-debt themselves.

What I would like to see is some equity and continuity of involvement in the Club from the Italian Community, to have them participating in the Club in great numbers. I would like to see them call meetings to discuss the problems of the Club; make them feel important for belonging to the Club. For instance, create conferences debating the needs of the community and to create the opportunity for people to feel useful, to be fulfilled. When I said that we are losing the values, those are the values that we are losing.

People ask me, what is the benefit of the Club? Well, I say, people always frequented the Club. But now, it's a bit like going into the casino with the hundreds of poker machines in there, that are always full. Then, there are other gambling initiatives, and people talk about a car they won in a raffle! AHHH! You are joking. I can see that you have to have progress and create things ... but still.

Don't lose your values. Progress with values.

The values that the Club was built on were for the Italian community in Australia to be a body of people with culture, prestige, and very sound values. Nowadays, things of that nature are not considered deeply enough to make an impact within the community.

What are the things that you take away with you from your experiences with the Club? What are the most poignant things, that your life experience with Club Marconi has given you?

Well, my experiences with Club Marconi have allowed me the opportunity to mix with so many people. I really enjoyed that element. I have also really enjoyed the functions that we used to put on. For example, we had the annual debutantes' ball. We had other festivities at the Club. At all of these functions, we invited the clergy to participate.

It is no longer the practice of involving the clergy to participate in things. And I wonder why this is. Don't the Australian population consider us Italians to be Catholics? Do we perform as Catholics?

If I asked you what you believe you will take away with you from the Club, what would that be?

My experience with Club Marconi has involved mixing with the Italians, Australians, and all the different communities in the area. Through the sports and everything else, I had the occasion to meet with all the different nationalities of the area. I would say that my participation with and working with all these different groups and, in particular, with the Italians, gave me a chance to evaluate people's minds and people's ways of thinking. I learnt to appreciate and respect the wishes of everyone; I learnt the fact that my way of thinking wasn't the only (correct) way of thinking. That it could, in fact, be something else. And there are other things to believe and do, but personally I would like to keep living my own way.

I also look at all the people who are not involved in the church or in any community activity. I am not here to condemn them, I can only see how much better off they would be. My experiences in being involved and doing different things has been terrific. I consider getting involved to be really living and having a purpose.

In a nutshell, I learnt to appreciate everyone's view, and respect it. Even if they are contrary to my own beliefs and my own values, they deserve an acknowledgement and respect.

I think that by not participating and not doing those things, means you have taken the easy way out of everything. It is important to participate in community-based activities; that is really important.

CHAPTER SIX
Raising a Family

"I was very pleased and very happy to see that Rina and I had accomplished something so valuable."

Can you describe the link between the Club, and the community and your own family?

My link with the Club is something that was borne from a necessity to bring the Italian community into a locality where they had something to share with things in common. There are many traditions that have been left behind, and at that time, caused a lot of nostalgia.

Club Marconi, in a sense, was a second family to me. The purpose of a family is to create a structure in which to bring up children with the right values. I have tested out my own values, where a strong family is the key to building a strong society. I think that Club Marconi was erected and established on the fundamental principles of family life, therefore promoting a sound and better society.

The activities of the Club have always been focused on the family, society, and the needs of the Italian Australian community. These things have been promoted because of the belief and values that have been imparted to me in my young days, ones I still live by today.

How important to your life do you feel Club Marconi has been to you?

Club Marconi to me has been an outlet for my values, and I have worked very hard to implement those values in the Italian community. I have given support to different things I have considered important, for example, the Youth Centre.

The Youth Centre's goal was to embrace the children of our members and care for them. That was done very efficiently. We looked at the cultural side, and we thought we would establish a library, which we did. Unfortunately, our community was too busy with work, and raising families, so the library never had the success for which we hoped.

One thing I had promoted at Club Marconi was to preserve the Italian language amongst our children. The idea was raised to the committee to start having classes, and they accepted. We got the classes organised and the first teachers. They were, among others, Reverend Father Romano, and another gentleman by the name of Pelissari.

Then, in Sydney, the organisation, CO.AS.IT—the Association of Cultural Studies for the Italian Community (amongst other things)—started teaching the Italian language. But the first in our community was at Club Marconi.

What is the link you have with CO.AS.IT?

The link with CO.AS.IT came after for Club Marconi. When we were established with the Italian school, CO.AS.IT took over the classes and provided the teachers. The classes were held at public schools and no longer at the Club. At the Club, there was only private tuition for adults.

I was elected to be the representative of the Italian classes in the Fairfield area. CO.AS.IT gave me that assignment and my task was to distribute the literature for learning the Italian language.

Then, I was nominated to be the patron of the Italian classes in the area. With that role, I would visit the schools once or twice a month or more, depending on necessity.

If there were any complaints or anything, I would consult with the parents. I used to consult with the teachers, and CO.AS.IT and I organised some activities at Club Marconi with the students and their families. At the end-of-year functions, the officials of CO.AS.IT were invited to attend and to hand out the diplomas to the children.

There were some very prolific learners, not everyone, but an effort was made to bring about the Italian language. The Australian national anthem was sung at the beginning of the classes. They were teaching Italian, but always with that spirit that they were Australian. They were born here; they were Australians, and this was a particular addition to their knowledge of another culture. We were very successful with it.

Do you feel that events and programs such as the Youth Centre and Italian language classes have created a release for you and your values and your desire to do things for the community?

Yes, I do. I always liked to combine the community interests and the church. I think they go hand in hand.

How important is this connection between community and church to you?

The connection is very important because the church and the faith are very close to the family, to the raising of children, and the imparting of the right values to everyone. I thought Club Marconi could contribute in some way to this.

And you felt this was part of your role?

This was my purpose of being at the Club, the promoting of different sports and different activities, which there were many. Early on, we had to consider expanding. We had to consider so many things that became necessary for the growth of the Club. We worked according to the finances.

We bought some land, which proved to be very essential in those days. The present and past committees found that very useful because there was room for expansion. We always dreamed that the Club would be big one day. We had visions for the Club, but of course I must admit that it was never envisaged to the extent that it has developed today.

What does the word, family, mean to you?

The word, family, means everything. I have always considered family an essential part of being a human being, an essential part of society, and one that I will always cherish. When I married, I really looked forward to the time when my family would start to be created, and the excitement attached to it; that feeling is something that I can't describe.

Despite the limited means, as a young married man, I had to provide for the family. I did so with confidence that I was able to give them a good education, to dress them. This was done together with my wife, of course. She is the giver of life; she gave me the family, and that is wonderful.

Who is your family? Who do you describe as your family?

My family begins with my wife and then my two sons and two daughters. I feel confident to say that we have imparted the values that were given to my wife and me.

Rina and I found so many things in common in each other that it cannot be described. We had the same values about family. I remember we were only three months married, and my good wife wanted to have a baby. It did eventuate, and that was a wonderful thing for us. It was a wonderful thing too for my mother and father, the grandparents. They were always looking forward to having grandchildren, and in fact, I remember this episode when we had our first one. I told my father, whose name was Guiseppe (Joseph), "Father, we have decided to call our first son Joseph."

He was so delighted he couldn't believe it; he thought we did a great thing. He used to do so much for the children. He used to cherish them, he used to play with them, talk to them. The children used to be all huddled around him and really listen to him.

Do you feel being the eldest has affected your understanding of roles and responsibility to family?

Well, the fact is I have always had to be responsible for my family. I had to be a responsible person from the age of twelve because of the circumstances in which I grew up in Italy. My situation demanded devotion to the family. Being the eldest, I can remember I had to change nappies quite often. I had to help to take the children to the doctors, because my brothers were getting too big for my mother and grandmother to carry.

Then, there were the animals to attend to, the farm to look after, and all of its problems. The corn had to be milled, the wheat and flour to be collected, firewood to be provided, and all of these things.

Do you think the responsibility that you had to take on taught you the notion of family responsibility very acutely?

Yes, and very early on.

And that has stayed with you?

It has stayed with me even till today. I don't regret the hardships of those days because they were hardships, but it was not all the time. We had enough to eat, and we used to make do. Even having to make do with everything was an experience and added value to my way of thinking.

And you feel the effect of those hardships you endured as a twelve-year-old impacted you when you had your own family?

Oh yes, my upbringing impacted how I brought up my own children.

Did you have a firm idea that you didn't want your own children to have the kind of responsibility that you had?

Yes, fortunately enough, they never had to go through the same things that I did. I was very happy and thankful that they were able to live in a much better atmosphere, here in Australia.

They had beds, and they were always clean and washed, and ready for school. Everything was taken care of, and I thought that was very different from what I had. Even though, at the beginning of our married life, to provide for the family was very hard because I never had conveniences.

I used to have a horse to plough the fields, and I used to carry water on my shoulders to water plants. But of course, it gave me the opportunity to show my children how I used to do things and, from time to time, I used to ask for their help to 'drop plants' and things like that.

Do you think that the responsibilities that you had as a child were harsh?

Well, looking back now, I would say that my upbringing was very hard.

Unfair?

No, not unfair, because there was no better way. If there was a better way, we never had the means to provide it. We had to work to create those means. Finally, we succeeded in doing that. I finished up buying a vehicle, a rotary hoe, a hand wheel, and I bought some land.

But when you were a boy, when you were twelve, do you think that the responsibilities you had were harsh?

Oh no, they were part of living, in those times. It was a common thing everywhere, except where there were big families. But we were alone. Dad provided a house, and we lived in it. We never had relatives with us. You see, it was customary to have from ten, up to fifteen people living together, at that time. The boys in those big families never had to do the things that I had to, because they had girls and women to help. In my case, Mum used to depend on my brothers and me.

Did you feel hard done by?

No, no, no one was hard done by.

Your loyalty to your family, your children, and grandchildren is so deep. I would like to ask you to go back and really think about how this came to be? How did your parents teach you the importance of family? And build in you your idea of family?

Well, that was the mode of living in our society, it was just accepted. It wasn't something that was imparted or imposed. The necessity was there and there was no alternative; we had to do it. Sometimes, I used to demonstrate to my family that instead of doing the work, I could have been playing and doing something else, but nevertheless, I learnt to be obedient and do what I was told.

What type of things would your father say to you in relation to family?

My father used to talk to me like a father but also a friend, and sometimes, I found myself taking advantage of his generosity of expression. For instance, one time in Italy, I was cutting some grass with a scythe. My father was very pleased with my job, and he was praising me for the work that I had done. He was giving me praise for one thing and the other and he said, "Well, you have been very good, so today (it was Sunday morning) at 10 o'clock, you can go to mass with the bike."

That was a reward. But I took advantage of that; I did go to church with the push bike, but I also went to see friends about five kilometres away. When I came back, it was later than they expected. I was reprimanded. I felt very, very hurt because I thought that I was a big fellow, and I was very important. I thought I was entitled to go and see my friends and that my father wouldn't mind. But I learnt differently, I didn't obey. I disobeyed, and that was a lesson.

When you joined your father in Australia, you gave all your money to him, until you were married. When was this decided?

I was very conscious of my family, and I knew that my father had another four children and a wife. He also had debts in Italy and debts here and he wanted to bring the family out here to Australia to be united again. So, putting my money in for the common use and goal was spontaneous! I didn't think anything of it. I used to bank it with my bankbook, and I surrendered my money to my father because there was a need.

But my father used to say to me when I went out, "Have you got any money?"

"No."

"What?" He would object. "Do you mean you are going to go out without money?"

So, he would give me five pounds or ten pounds to 'put in my wallet'.

"You don't have to spend it, but you must have it in your wallet," he would advise.

You never took advantage of it?

No, I never spent it unnecessarily. I never did. Then he would ask me again about it. "No, I still got some," I would say, and he was happy with that because it showed I was a responsible person, and he could trust me with everything. And that is how family life developed.

What part does your faith play in your understandings of commitment and responsibility to your family?

Faith influenced me a lot. Faith was what my parents, my relatives, and the whole townspeople brought me up with. They were all churchgoers; they were all attending ceremonies at church, at mass, and of course, we used to go to Sunday School.

At Sunday School, they used to impart teachings that are valuable today without question. Teachings about family life and obedience and about being fair with God. In it were fundamental principles and values that are still with me today.

When you married, did your notions of family change? Did you think 'things are really different from this point of view now that I'm the husband'?

When I was courting Nanna, we often got onto this subject; we would talk about family life, what we liked and didn't like. Also, what was expected of me, and what I expected of her. All of these things came together, and we found ourselves getting married in good harmony. We shared everything that we came across. I would say, "I don't expect you to come and work on the farm. You look after the house." But from the first week, she came and joined me on the farm, and I'd say, "But you don't have to do this."

"No, no," she replied. She wanted to be there with me, she wanted to be part of 'the whole marriage parcel'. That is what I call family building.

Making sacrifices for the better good?

Yes, we both made sacrifices for everything. We always went to church, and we always brought our children to church. The priest used to come and see us and have a meal with us and the children used to listen to him. Father Cletis was one of them.

When the children were growing up, I became aware of their fondness for music and dancing, so we ended up buying a stereo.

We bought the stereo, but then you needed friends to listen with. So, the house was always full of friends, Australian friends, schoolmates, girls, and boys. They used to dance and sing, play, and joke, but always with those values, those principles. They always maintained these values; there was no mucking around. Rina wouldn't have tolerated it, anyway.

What does it mean to you to be a father?

Well, I always believed that we are put in this world to procreate and for me to become a father, I thought was a present from God. I was very pleased and very happy to see that Rina and I had accomplished something so valuable.

When the fourth child came along, Maria, we really felt that our family was completed. We strived very hard to educate them and give them things that we never had the joy of having.

We all enjoyed each other's company, our family, our music, and our outings. At one stage, when I bought the truck, we used to all fit in the front, but bit-by-bit, we couldn't manage anymore. So, what we did is we put a two-seater lounge at the back of the truck for the boys. When we would go out for picnics in different areas, I really felt like I was the 'King of the World'. Beside me was my wife and my family. I thought that I was really living!

Then, we would all stop and have dinner, kick a ball, have a bit of fun and things like that.

Now possibly, I could ask you a question. You see how our two boys live—Joe and Arthur—their principles and their values. Is this not evidence? Now, my girls, Pauline and Maria, their values, you see in them again, the good values. So, there are, when we humans become parents, we must have the knowledge and the right values to impart to the new generation, to our offspring. We must have those things. If you don't have them, and you follow the trends of the world, then you lose your purpose in life.

Do you see your role as a father, as your purpose in life?

My role as a father? I can't say I was absolutely perfect, but I would have liked to be very much so. Sometimes, I found myself reprimanding my children in a very severe way; perhaps that was unnecessary. Nevertheless, it was important because they got to know my temperament. I also got to know their feelings and how they felt when I got upset.

What do you believe your role was and is as a father to your children?

My role as a father was to impart my knowledge and values to them so they learnt to love and appreciate me. But I also knew that for that to happen, I would in fact have to consider them and their feelings and not be indifferent to their feelings toward me or towards my argument.

What about educating them?

I always strived and pushed them to do well at school. When Joe and Arthur wanted to leave school, I was really disappointed because I wanted them to stay at school. We managed to convince Joe to go to Year 12, but Arthur wouldn't have any part of it. Nevertheless, I knew they were really hard workers; they weren't larrikins.

Our boys know how to live and respect everybody; they are liked by everybody and that's what has always pleased us. They used to bring their friends to our place, and we used to accept their friends and join in with them. That is what family life should be.

You said before that, at some points, you severely reprimanded your children. Do you have any regrets in your fatherhood?

No regrets. Like I said before, I didn't convince the boys in particular to continue studying. We sent them to Parramatta (NSW) to the Marist Brothers, and there they were in the cadets. They were very proud of wearing the uniform and we felt proud ourselves to see them with the uniform on. They used to go camping in Singleton near Maitland, there was a big military camp there. There they had army officials giving tuition on guns and they used to go shooting.

Joe became a sergeant, and he was a good shot. But you see, being part of this, they were not belligerent. Their training was far from belligerent because they used to talk to them. They told them to be proud of their uniform, proud of the nation that they are part of. They used to say, "One day, we may be called to defend our country," and of course, it may be them. We are very proud of them, and they used to socialise with different men and, of course, that made them very sociable.

Even today, they are still bumping into their old school friends, and they talk about Singleton. They talk about the sport, the football, and the ankles they twisted.

Do you think that you have been successful as a father looking at your children?

Yes, I feel I have been successful as a father.

Because of their values?

Yes, very successful, very happy about the values that Rina and I have instilled.

Because their values are important to you?

Values are very important because I know that they stand in society with their heads up and there are no regrets. There are no bad names or bad doings, there is none of that. So, what else could a father want? In fact, I would say what else would parents want?

In this discussion, I should always include my wife because without her, I definitely would have been a different father, too. When I used to get 'off my block' a bit, my wife reminded me. She would say, "Eh, calm down, would you?"

Would you change anything if you could go back in time?

Well, the only thing that I would change is my education. I would like the opportunity to be better educated. I would have liked to have played an instrument, to have a greater knowledge than what I have at the present about literature, arts, and everything that I missed because I never had time.

People used to say, "Why don't you come down to the Club and have a game of cards?"

I would reply, "How can I?" I never learnt to play, I never had time to. In the same token, I don't regret it because I didn't waste my time. I was more constructive with better values. I wasn't selfish, because if I was selfish, I would have said, "Oh blow them!" but I could never do that to my family, never! Not for a single moment. They always come first. Rina was exactly the same.

What did it feel like when you became a grandfather?

Well, to become a grandfather; that was something. It was a repeat of the feelings I had when we had Joe, our first son. When I went to see Joseph in hospital, I had a guard accompanying me as it was during World War 2.

I remember Adrian, our first grandchild, in his first few months. He had a problem with eczema on the skin and used to be very restless. I remember going over to Joe and Esterina's (Joe's wife) house with Rina, and I got Adrian in my lap and took him for a ride around the district. I was trying to break his monotony.

You know I really feel for this generation, our grandchildren. Sometimes, I am embarrassing because I ask a lot of questions, but I want to see things and I want to know and understand what their life is like. But I ask questions and challenge them, without malice. If I disagree with them, it is because my values were different, and that is what my values still are. And I would like to be present, to be a witness to their lives. I want to be part of their lives.

When you became a grandfather again and again and again—thirteen times, in fact—did it ever affect your notions of where you were at your stage in life?

I will tell you this much—I was very grateful to God to be able to see all the thirteen grandchildren all well, healthy, and normal. That was a great thing to be thankful for.

I always enjoyed their presence, as they grew up, and when their birthdays came along or when their little events used to come around, that gave us the opportunity to give them something and see them appreciate the little things. Oh, that gave us great pleasure. We appreciate it immensely to have the means to contribute to their happiness.

It didn't have any other effects for you about where you are in your life stage?

Actually, I used to boast about it. Four children, all married, and thirteen grandchildren. Recently, I took Nanna to physiotherapy, and we got talking to a lady about one thing and the other and I said, "You know what, we are great-grandparents two times already, and we may be four times before the year is out!"[24] So you see, we can't be indifferent to the welfare and happiness of our offspring.

Now your children have children of their own, what do you believe your role is now? Has it changed?

Well, I feel very lucky to have been able to support my grandchildren financially when they started off in married life and after.

Perhaps your role now was to be more of a father, in a different way, to your children because they now have children of their own?

Oh, for sure. I have to accept the fact that the advice I give my sons and daughters about their children is different to theirs. I could express my views. I feel that perhaps in certain fields they haven't made the right decisions, and amends could be made, but of course you are not always in agreement. I can understand that, because I am not living with the grandchildren, they are. I don't know what passes between them; therefore, I can give a judgement, but I can't be in a position to judge. Overall, I must accept and hope and treat the grandchildren normally without any difference.

---

[24] In 2023, Felice and Rina had twenty-six great-grandchildren

For instance, we have Catherine, we have Jerome, we have you (to be truthful), who have perhaps deviated from the norm. We say, well they are living in a different era, their circumstances are not the same, their values may not be the same either, so I can't blame anybody. The thing that remains is this: our grandchildren are our grandchildren, and we are very proud, and we are going to do everything to make them happy and to see them happy. That is the main thing.

So, the rest I will leave aside, because you have to live with a person to know him and you can't be in a position to judge.

Do you think you have more in common with your own children when they became parents?

Well, yes. You see, I felt that my authority and my values had been instilled, and from then on, it was up to them.

So, you are passing the baton to them?

Yes, and they can pass the baton to their offspring.

I will tell you something else, at this stage.

My brothers are very diverse in character. We had Davino, and we had Louie. Louie was a different character to all of us, but we understood each other, so much so that when he was sick, he wrote about me. And he left it to his wife, like a diary. He had only words of praise for me. That is how it was, but he never got on with Dad. They used to clash; he was very strong-minded, and he thought things in his own way. I was going to say, much like in the same way as you do (referring to Felicity).

But he was really determined in that way. And I used to say, "Compromise, please!" But he wouldn't want to.

You were the middleman, were you?

I was the middleman of the family with everything. And of course, what Dad couldn't do for Rina and me, in particular. He used to love Rina; I can't believe how much he used to think of Rina. Getting back to what we said before, about acknowledging and accepting, I have had these experiences, and I was the middleman.

What do you believe your role as a grandfather is directly related to your grandchildren?

Well, like I said before, my grandchildren have gone on to have their own lives. They have developed their own values. Not only the values that their parents imparted, but the values that they learnt due to circumstances in their life. There have been changes to the world, the circumstances of how they are growing up are extremely different to my experiences.

So, as a grandparent, the only thing that I wish to see is happiness for my grandchildren. The part that I can play is very limited because I cannot express myself without determination. I have to be tactful, and I have to be understanding of what I say because it may not be considered in line with today's values. In that way, I am a bit restricted. Not that I feel hurt about it, not that I don't like the children because they don't think the way I do, far from it. That has nothing to do with it. I appreciate the opportunity to express my ideas and to hear their voices and their opinions and then I can evaluate the difference between today and yesterday.

So, you believe your role as a grandparent is not a parenting role; it is more of a supportive, bit more in the background, but an important presence in their life?

I feel that my grandchildren respect both of us, myself and my wife and I feel they know that we care for them very much. That is all we want and hope for. There is no more we can do ...

What do you believe you have gotten out of being a parent? How has it enriched or changed your life?

Being a parent, (and I hope you have the experience one day), is the ambition to have your children educated and to have them love you. This is not only because you are their parent, but because of your values and what you have imparted to them. Of course, that fills one with ego, pride, and achievement, surrounded by understanding and love. What else can I say?

So, it has made you feel good about yourself?

It has made me feel absolutely wonderful!

You like who you are when you are being a parent?

That is right. Of course, there is always room for improvement. Sometimes, I wish I could have been better, but that is not something that I could see to be immediately necessary. Perhaps I don't know how to be better. Now, I accept things as they are.

What do you believe are the differences in the roles between a mother and a father?

Well, that is a very, very important subject. First of all, I must tell you that the mother is the builder of a family. The mother is the builder of harmony who imparts intuition, principles, and faith. The role of a husband is to second her and to help her in that field. If I was negative about what the mother is, my wife's values, and go against her, then you wouldn't create a family.

Like I said before, the wife is the founder of a family, and the family is the founder of society. According to the values of her, you build a society. You see, that is how things work. Nobody could tell me any different because I am thoroughly convinced of it.

So, maybe it is a good time to ask you this question: how important is a family to an individual's personal, spiritual, and physical development?

Well, I can only talk through experience. I find myself begging God to help me in difficulties that I come across, whether financial or in any field at all. I find that faith has helped me immensely.

Another thing I learnt by reading is that human beings, by nature, believe there is a supernatural. It doesn't matter how; it doesn't matter what. Indigenous people of all countries, they all have that feeling that there is somebody above them. Now, I am not able to debate whether that is a spiritual phenomenon or whether it is the make-up of the genes of the human being, because I didn't study enough to be specific on this matter, but I know what it does for me.

I believe that I have done something with help from the one I call God, that otherwise would not have been possible. You see, I was brought up that way and I am used it. I am not ashamed to say that I found myself praying to God to help with this and that. I prayed to Him once to get the consent to marry my wife. There were things of that nature. I prayed to God to have children, and they came; and to have them all healthy and that they all are, I felt blessed. All of these things! How could I be indifferent? I am very grateful!

How important is having a family around someone? If you look at any individual, how important do you think family is to any individual's life?

Well, I will put it to you this way: from my experience, I have seen couples that have lost ties with their families; they are not interested. They reckon they are not wanted. They state, "Oh well, they will manage. They managed better than I did. Oh, they are all right." They don't worry about it.

I could say the same thing. "What do I need my children for? What for? The children around me, what do I do with them?" Or, I could say, "Go to hell. I will go my own way. Let's pick up my bags and I will go my way, never mind about them."

Those people have nothing! There is nothing there! There is nothing in your heart, there is nothing in your mind to do that. You can't!

My son, Joe, travelled to Japan, but first, he came here and said goodbye. That touched me very deeply. He said, "Goodbye Dad."

I replied, "Goodbye Son, take care of yourself."

Your dad (Arthur) rang me this afternoon, and he asked, "How are you all? Are you alright?" What can I say but thank you very much for ringing? I feel that closeness from my son. For my sons to feel close to me, I can't help but feeling close to them. That is what you call family life.

If you become indifferent to little, stupid things that might be said, and cut me out because he said this and the other … come on! Why? What for?

Another thing with my character; if I have a friend and all of a sudden—boof! —he is not a friend anymore. Well, I could say, "Oh well, he can go to buggery," but not me.

I go and ask him, "Did I do anything wrong to you, because if I did, I am here to apologise, tell me."

You see, I have to do that. It is who I am.

How important do you think families are to a society and to a political sphere?

Parents cannot impose their will on a grown-up son or daughter. You must respect their individuality and their wishes. I could go out of my way to express my views on certain subjects, but I feel if they don't accept my views, too bad. I won't hold it against them, not on my life. Only time will prove whether you are right, or I am right.

I want you to talk about how you believe that family is vital to a successful society.

Here we go, back to values. The values created in a family are the values that should be provided in society. Once the society gets away from the family values, you don't have a healthy society or community. You have people that steal; you have people that rob you; people that are antagonistic; people that indulge in drinking; and other things of that nature.

That is why family is so important. Parents should show the way; there are no two ways about it. If I was a drunk, how could I expect to face my children and say to them, "Hey, you've had enough to drink …" I didn't have to do that in my life because they have never seen me drunk. The only thing that I abused was smoking and unfortunately, they took up smoking too. That is the only vice that I had and when I gave it up, they gave it up too.

They asked me once, "Why do you smoke so much?" And I answered, "I am frightened that I will get too old. I am smoking cigarettes so they can kill me." They understood what I meant. It was a moment for me, to say that. I saw the look in their eyes. After that, I gave it away.

How do you feel about your broader family, your brothers, and your cousins? What is your role as a brother now? We talked about how hard you had to work to bring them over here and you supported them financially with your father. What is your role now?

This is becoming a very personal subject. The closeness to my brothers has always been the same. I have always felt it. When my brothers left home, they didn't telephone to find out how I was, and I wondered why. *They must be busy*, I pondered. This occurs within families, not only my brothers.

All of your brothers married a long time ago, didn't they?

Yes, they married a long time ago, but their feelings, our friendship, the togetherness, the closeness ... this all dims when this takes place. Now perhaps, they think the same in my position, because I am in the same position — married with a family.

When we were single, we went together all the bloomin' time. Then, when we got married, everyone got busy forming their own family, and they all had to compromise.

Is this what you have done?

Yeah, I have had to compromise with everything, but for the main thing, my brothers and I are still close. We are still very close.

My brothers are my brothers. As the eldest child, I cleaned their bottoms, changed their nappies; they didn't change mine! I took them out for walks; I carried them to the doctors, and I carried them home. I also took them to Sunday School and *Azilo* (preschool). I think that they should remember me. It is only recently I don't feel too well, and they also don't feel too well themselves, which makes it difficult to keep in touch ...

If you could give a message to the country on families, what would you say in light of your own thoughts on the topic?

Well, I had an occasion to say something about this not that long ago, in public. I said, "I admire the continuity that is made up of the family values because we must realise that civilisation derives from family values. If we want to have a society that is worthy and appreciative, we must have the right values. You, as parents, have the duty to impart these values and be responsible for the children, not to put them in this world and expect society to mind them; that is very wrong."

Thankfully, that sentiment was understood and appreciated very much.

How was it for you when your father died? Did it change your experiences of family? Did you have to take on more responsibility for the family when he died?

Well, with my father passing away ...

Can you just elaborate on the circumstances of his death?

Well, he was sick for quite a while. He used to play bowls at the Merrylands Bowling Club. He was a good player and, in fact, when he passed away, there were representatives from the Bowling Club that attended his funeral. That made us very pleased and proud of my dad.

After he passed away, we were left with Mum. Dad had shifted into a small property in Perceval Road, Smithfield. There he had a garden and a small cottage, and he had his tool shed in which he used to potter around. He used to love his garden, his roses and his flowers. He used to keep things very, very tidy. He was a very proud person about his garden and everything else.

While he was well, he used to come down to my place and help with anything I needed. Dad would even go as far as to say, "Leave it, I'll do that, I will come and do it for you." You can just imagine. I really needed help because of the four children and having to provide for them.

Without electricity and water pipes, it was very hard, carrying water on my back to water plants and things like that. We had to heat the water in the copper and pass it through the window into the bathroom.

Anyway, getting back to Dad, after his passing, we had Mum, and she was on her own in the house. We didn't think that was fair, so Arthur used to go and sleep in the house when he was single. And it finished up that she was suffering with her legs. She complained to our parish priest, Father Berra, about her condition as she didn't want to trouble us because we used to take Mum for a month, each of us.

She didn't fancy that moving-around-between-children system too much because of her legs and we had four children, and Rina was pressed; every one of us was pressed. When you get married and have kids, that is how it is. Anyway, she convinced this Father Berra to find a place for her and he did.

He came over one day and said to me, "Phil, you mother has asked me to provide a resting place for her and I did find such a place. Why don't you be reasonable and give her what she wants? This time in her life, she is entitled to it."

Well, it simply took my entire ego away. I simply realised what he said could be true. She didn't want to be a burden on our families. She wanted to be independent! Well, alright I thought. So, it finished up that we made an appointment for her to enter a retirement village. Anyway, I took her there and the first thing we did was go to the chapel there, this little church. Mum wanted to go there. She was delighted because they had a church in the same locality. I took her to her room, and I said, "Mum, you don't have to stay here, you know." The next day I went back there, and she said, "Oh, no, I am staying here."

Mum befriended Mrs Martinelli and another Italian lady, and she was happy. But she was always suffering with her legs. We tried doctors and specialists, what we didn't try to make her comfortable is nobody's business!

Then Mrs Martinellli went to Brisbane and the other lady took sick. Mum didn't have any close friends that could speak her own language, so we took her to the Scalabrini Village. That is where she spent her last few days.

Did she like it there?

Oh yeah, she liked it there alright, but she became very sick and dependent for everything. She started to go down and down in her health and she got thinner and thinner. She was almost ninety when she died.

How did it affect you when she died?

I felt so sad when she died. I can describe it like this: if you went out into the garden and cut a rose which is in full bloom, and you take it inside and put it into a vase and then the petals fall off. I felt that I really lost something very, very valuable. My mother used to be a very caring woman. What she didn't do for us was nobody's business! As children, she cared for our cleanliness, insisting on our prayers at night and morning, and all those things. She was a terrific mother; she was terrific! Yep.

What lessons of life did you learn from your parents?

Well, to answer this question, I will have to repeat myself. What I learnt from my parents is to respect everybody, to be nice, and not to get into trouble. One has to respect everybody as you would respect yourself and do the best you can to stand out in the world, in society, at school, and church, and to give the best example.

I know that when my brother and I performed our little part at the preschool and in the church play, oh, my parents were really…. you know proud, that was really something great that they witnessed. Of course, all of these little things stay in your mind.

What about their personalities? What sticks out for you that you would like to share?

My father's personality? Well, he was a very talented person. He could do anything with his hands and was very intelligent. He would debate his point of view and 99% of the time, he was right in his estimations.

During the war (they never had the chance to be educated, they never went to school or anything), when he went to the army, he started to learn and pick up things, like writing a few words, because he wanted to write to his wife at home. He began to write and understand so much that he was commissioned to build a building with a company of 150 men. The major asked who was willing to do the construction and everything. There were others and he didn't have any skills before, but he did it. Then he advanced, and he became a driver of an anti-air cannon, and they managed to shoot down a German plane. They were awarded a holiday for their achievement.

But at home on the farm, everything had to be precise, as he was a perfectionist. We would go to plant things, and they had to be marked because they had to be precise. We had a string line, and we put a mark of black paint at certain distances along the string. Then, we would then run the string and plant where the mark was. When you finished planting, everything was square where the mark was; everything was square one way and square the other way. This is where Louie used to go mad! "What is the use of this? Let's just plant the damn things!" He would say ... (laughter). "Just plant them at every step."

Dad was a perfectionist at everything—with the tools, the horses, the plough—everything. We had to work according to his specification. He used to do things with his hands, such as make flower stands and baskets. He also had a photographic memory: he would see a thing, memorise it, and build it. That was him. He built a shed for Terry with timber and railway sleepers, standing up without putting them in the ground. He bound them up and put a roof on it and everything. Nothing could shift it. He was simply like that.

What were your parents like together?

Oh, my parents were quite compatible. Dad was always the boss. In those days, that was how it was. When they were walking somewhere, Dad would be in front and Mum behind. They were a bit shy to show affection in front of the children, and that was something that was reserved between them and nothing to do with anyone else.

How did your father feel about having so many boys and no girls!

He was delighted. Oh, he was so delighted! He used to joke and say, "I had five of them and the five of them had the same thing! I was looking for something different, but it was never there." (laughs).

CHAPTER SEVEN
Faith and Politics

*"Well, we mightn't have found the answer,
but are we supposed to?
We have teachings that date back thousands of years;
We have experiences that have lasted from years ago;
We have discoveries that are there to tell us there is
something above us."*

I want to ask you about the family picnics that you organised. What were the motivations behind them?

I'm privileged to say that of all people, I was looked upon to be the President of Club Marconi. It gave me the opportunity to organise things, and I was able to do something for our community. Not only our family but also for the community. I've always been very fond, patriotic, and nostalgic about *Sesto al Reghena* my native town, and I wanted to organise a picnic for people to get together who were from the same region[25]. I promoted these picnics, and they were always successful.

We held the first picnic at Club Marconi, we've even got photos of it. Sadly, some of the people are no longer with us, but the atmosphere of these picnics was fantastic. We would reminisce ... living a little of our past, living a little of our town, and bringing up our own customs and traditions. These picnics were very successful, so much so that we proposed to have one every year. We went to different places for these picnics where we provided some activities like tug-o-war and races, particularly for the children. The children used to love it. About 150-200 people would come on different occasions.

---

[25] Sesto al Reghena is a Province of Pordenone, Italy, approximately 77 km northeast of Venice.

Can you describe your feelings of nostalgia towards *Sesto*?

Well, you see, this is something you've got to experience to really know what it means. What you feel is not very easy to put into words. Academically speaking, I'm not able to, but I can really say the memories of my youth in Italy make me nostalgic, as it does to others. The memories of our school days, of going to church, going to Sunday School, receiving Confirmation, Holy Communion, the clothes, the preparations, and the multitude of the people that used to attend these masses, ceremonies, processions and different occasions, the recurrence of Saints, Mary Immaculate, St Anthony and so forth, are all memories of my childhood that I cherish. There was a procession that was followed by the whole town - the bells would ring in a festive way; people would be calling out to each other. Everything was very special. They were the things we used to do and the things we used to experience.

The first time I went back to Italy, I took a tape recorder, and I recorded messages from different families that we met there. Once I returned, I got everyone together here, and we played them the tape. I had the voices of their parents, uncles, brothers, and everyone had a chance to hear what they had to say.

I also recorded the bell from our tower and the mass that was sung on special occasions. Every year in the town, they had a Feast of the Migrants in August. In Europe, there seems to be a universal holiday, where everybody gets back to their home on the 15th of August, which is the recurrence of the Feast of the Madonna. On this day in *Sesto*, the council used to provide a little refreshment, and the mayor would say a few words, followed by the parish priest, who would bless all those that were present. Of course, all these things, you know, we missed once we emigrated to Australia. When we had the picnics, most of the time, we organised for a mass to be held with it, but it wasn't always possible. Nevertheless, this provided an opportunity for all of us to recall those occasions and share those feelings and events.

When did the picnics start?

The first picnic was in 1964, with the last picnic being held in 1986 at Villawood. That was very good going; twenty-two years. I had books with records and minutes with the participants' names and I even had a bank account made out to this gathering of Sestenci.

Of course, organising such things takes its toll, and unfortunately, if it wasn't for me pushing for these things, no one else seemed to want to take it up. But when I wanted to take them up, everybody would respond and attend and participate.

I handed everything to my relative, Elio Zadro, hoping that he would keep it up, but he was too busy with the family. He has a large family who have now grown up, so there were always weddings and engagements, people going and coming, the subdivision of his land, and the building of his house. All of these things take time and disrupt the social side of things in the community.

What was it like getting together with all the people from *Sesto*? Did you know everyone from *Sesto*, or did you meet them here?

I knew all the families and so, I knew most people. I can't say I knew all their offspring, the ones who were born here.

In fact, if I was to meet them now, I wouldn't know them, and they wouldn't know me because we haven't met for a while.

That was another purpose of uniting and having these picnics—we had a chance to meet everyone's offspring, nephews, cousins, and so forth, and keep the connection going. Now, all of that has fallen by the wayside and, unfortunately, I'm not enjoying the health and vitality that is necessary to have these things going right.

As far as my religion, well, you can just imagine, that was something that had the priority over everything. I remember in our family, of an evening, after our last meal, we would all get around the table and say the Rosary.

You would say the Rosary with your own family or when you were younger, when you were with your parents?

Saying the Rosary, that's how we grew up with our family. But even before that, when my father was with his brothers, my grandmother, and their wives, that was the tradition.

Can you describe the basis of your faith? If someone asked, "What is your faith? What do you believe in?", what do you say?

That's a fundamental thing, and a very important question. I do believe my parents taught me the benefits of believing, the advantages of believing, and the importance of faith.

I had some experiences; I think I spoke to you before of Merriwa? I have reason to believe that my faith helped me a great deal in my first days in Australia. I remember travelling up a mountain because I thought I was close to my country and that I could see further away.

From there, on top of those hills, I sang aloud. I enjoyed the echo of my voice from the hills. I thought I was so gifted by God, with my faith and everything. I must say that I was brought up to say my prayers morning and evening, and I kept that up for a very long time. Now, I limit myself to thinking about my religion and my faith in God. I believe God gave me the gift of my family and getting married. I married my wife, who has the same religion, principles and values; in particular, family values.

My wife and I got on very well and were lucky to have children. I think we were gifted and that we still are gifted by God. All our kids are beautiful and intelligent, and having our grandchildren, who are all very successful in life with studies and everything.

Now, we have great grandchildren popping up everywhere. To look at them, we see their beauty, the gift of God. We feel like God really gifted us with all of these wonderful things. Rina and I pray for our family; that they will keep those values alive and proceed in a way that is creative and that they lead a life of principle.

Of course, life today is changing. It is changing so fast. Today's values are limited in comparison to our own values. They seemed to divert to a different line, and everything seems to be accepted.

In fact, to hear governments acknowledge the fact that children have rights over parents, and that teachers have no rights on children, and that parents and teachers cannot chastise a child to the extent that a child could challenge them ... well, that is totally foreign to our way.

The way we were born, the way we were taught, and the way we reasoned; today, it is all topsy-turvy. In my opinion, this is something that we have lost and unfortunately, society will have to pay for it in the long run. What kind of world is developing around us? We are witnessing all of this and can't do anything about it. We only pray that God will perhaps enlighten the responsible persons, the teachers, the government, or the clergy, to adopt and maintain the way of the world.

Why is your faith and religion so important to you?

Religion is very important to me because I feel that in religion, I can find the fundamentals necessary for life. It is these fundamentals, the ones that I was saying before, that seem to have devalued; they are not so important anymore.

Can you name the fundamentals of life?

Well, I would have to generalise on this subject. Governments, teachers, and administrators seem to be completely indifferent to honesty and morality; a different concept of life seems to have been accepted. So much so that we have courts that gaol people for twenty-five years, and the next thing, they let them out early because they, according to their own principle, behave themselves in gaol.

You think those changes have to do with religion?

The lack of fundamentals and following through has to do with a lack of religion; lack of following the Ten Commandments.

Do you feel that religion has lost its grasp on society recently, or things have always been like this?

No, no, religion has lost its values because of the world that exists today. What I have experienced is this: with poverty or mediocre progress, people subscribe to God. When they get everything they need, and then one day they don't get what they want, they steal it. They must have it! So much so that society is corrupted.

Is that greed?

Yes, greed, and it comes from being spoilt. It is like having an apple today and a carrot tomorrow, but the carrot hasn't got the value of the apple. There are things to which I could finger point, but I will say that despite the *progress* around us, I think religion is coming back.

I think the youth of today have had so much of everything they wanted that now, I feel, they recognise there is something more worthwhile to live for. There is something else for them to enjoy that would give them a better conscience, a better life, a better future, and something to aspire to.

There was a period when there was no hope. No one seemed to be happy about anything. Everything seemed to be too much trouble, with people demonstrating against religion, demonstrating against nations, demonstrations everywhere. I believe this was all brought about because of corruption, and the kids are not to blame. It is the adults that have created a dysfunctional atmosphere for them.

Are you talking about a specific time or place?

Internationally speaking, there has not been a recent time of peace, and a child needs to grow up in a world of peace.

Dear oh dear! My father and my uncles went to the First World War, and that was to be the war that was supposed to end all wars. That was the conception of all politicians, but no, peace didn't last and why is that? Because one has to have everything, whilst the other one has nothing! Then, the one that has nothing has every right to revolt. That is where the corruption came in. Like I said before, we should follow the Ten Commandments. I consider them the basis of a healthy humanity. Unfortunately, it is not compulsory to follow the Ten Commandments, it would be too easy. Just imagine!

Now, we have to live our own way and indulge in all of the things that come before us and if they are not here, we look for them and strain for them; I don't think that is right. There are more important things, like striving for the welfare of a family, the welfare of our children, and our own welfare.

In your mind, is it the lack of imparting values, or is it the furnishing of children with luxuries, that is the problem?

My children had everything they wanted—toys, bikes, motorcars. They got to go to school and have all the facilities. There was a time that the fellow next door couldn't afford a bicycle or a proper pair of shoes to walk to school. See, those are the things that really justify life and yet, those things should not define your success; the difference in classes should not exist.

I know that it is impossible because of men's character. There are characters that would apply themselves and strive for wealth but not with values, because when you strive for wealth, it does not have everything that is necessary for life. You see? You find many people that the more wealth they have, the more corrupt they become. These are the things that I am confronted with, and which create a different and confused world.

Do you think there is room in your idea of a world that would include other religions, if they were still striving for goodness? Do you think that all religions are striving for the same goodness?

I would say, in a very big way, all religions are striving for betterment. There are some religions that were born out of Christianity, but they weren't happy with the Christian religion because it was subjecting people to things in a different way. I'm not here to condemn them; I would like to be in a learned position, to be able to debate these things. I've got my little way of describing them only.

My religion started with Jesus Christ and all the Christian religions are based on Christ. With Christianity, there are fundamental things that derive from the Ten Commandments. You will find that some religions take from the Ten Commandments but leave some things out because it does not suit them.

Some of them are responsive and promoted by people with different ideas to create a voice for themselves, so people will follow them, and they say extraordinary things.

If you remember a few years ago, there were many people who committed suicide in Texas, America.[26] A few months ago, in America again, they set fire to this building ... in the name of religion. All of these things are so confused, why is that?

Now, we have got this war in Serbia that want people that have been there for centuries, two, three hundred years or more, out of the territory because they aren't of a specific

---

[26] Waco, Texas, USA. On April 19, 1993, a Christian cult called the Branch Davidians, committed mass suicide through self-immolation after a 51-day siege with police. Seventy-five people died, including twenty-five children.

race. Why? Why should this occur? A war: it is all about killing, murdering, and destruction!

I say, "Hey!" Where do the Ten Commandments come in? What about the preaching of Christ that we all embraced? America embraced him. Even the dictator, Milošević himself, and he is supposed to be a Christian, an Orthodox. How can you kill people to bring your own beliefs in? With killing? War? Destruction? No.

Do you feel war and especially religious wars are events that we should learn from?

Exactly, we need to learn. In fact, the time has passed; it is overdue. We should have already learnt these lessons centuries ago. With war, we don't achieve anything. After all, we are all human beings; we are all in this world for one purpose and that is for procreating. And what are we doing? We are destroying one another.

How do you rationalise the war in Ireland that was a Catholic versus a Protestant conflict?

Catholic and Protestant are fundamentally, very similar religions.

They fight because one thinks he is better than the other and one doesn't accept the other. Where is the sense of that?

You see, the main problem—well, this is my interpretation of the problem—is that Ireland has become a British colony. Of course, parts of Ireland have retained their own sense of religion, created by Henry the Eighth, but part of Ireland was Catholic. In fact, St Benedict came from there. They embraced the Catholic religion, but the Protestants won't have them. Now they try to unite, and we see the Protestants making an effort, or the Catholics making an effort, but how can you solve that one if there isn't any compromise between them?

I had an occasion, not so long ago, to see a Protestant Priest and a Catholic Priest together. They were getting on fine together in terms of their religion and they were really friends. They were parish neighbours, and they were living side-by-side. You see, it is the politicians who are the bigots. The stubbornness of people on both sides, not accepting each other ... come on!

Do you feel like it is time to say, "Stop it!"

Enough is enough. Are we a civilised people or are we barbarians?

I want to get back to your opinions on the Catholic Church. Do you think that the Church must change to keep up with the world in which it exists? Do you think it must change on issues such as contraception? Married priests? Women priests? Or on the other issues that are controversial to the Church, and yet accepted in everyday societal life?

Yes, this is a very tricky question. A very important one. You see, the trend of today is caused by too much wealth and that is why it becomes necessary to look for alternatives. It is too hard the other way. Nobody wants to put up with anything that is excessively hard to comprehend or practice.

Do you think that wealth is the basis of changing attitudes away from the Church?

I find that with too much wealth, too many things are easy; there are too many enjoyments, and too much variety. We have a shortage of priests, and why? That is the question I should be able to answer. I have my own ideas of why, but my ideas are going back to what I said before. Everybody has everything too easy; everyone has become independent of God to achieve what he or she has in life. They say, "I don't need God, I can look after myself. I can do this. Why should I bother about God?" They ignore the fact that we are God's creation.

If one doesn't believe that, does it apply to them?

Oh no, they won't believe, they won't even contemplate it. But fact is fact! That's how it is for me. That's how the world began — creation and everything. Now with today's discoveries and today's technologies, they are digging up things that make you wonder, but by the same token, it makes you wonder how that could be possible without a beginning ... and who was the beginning?

Maybe we just haven't found the answer yet?

Well, we mightn't have found the answer, but are we supposed to? We have teachings that date back thousands of years, we have experiences that have lasted from years ago; we have discoveries that are there to tell us there is something above us.

We have learned that people say that, despite all this science and everything, human beings are in need of a superior being. You get the indigenous people of this Earth, and they themselves feel that they must come from somewhere, that there must be someone else above them, and they are very spiritual. When you are talking about spirituality, what are you connected to?

So, are you saying that it is a human trait to believe that there is something else, something superior to ourselves?

Yes, it is a human trait to believe that there is someone else, and I happen to read, and I hear knowledgeable people saying there is a God, there must be a Supreme Being. Then, you must ask yourself questions. "If there is a God, why do we get these typhoons or the destruction of homes or why do we have wars?" or "Why do we have things that are abnormalities?" You ask these questions. The destruction, disease, people dying on the roads? If there is a God that loves us, why should he subject us to this kind of thing? And yet it has always been, and that was answered, in a way, very satisfactorily, they were saying that God is a good God and He doesn't promote these kind of things. He does not punish anyone with the elements themselves, with cyclones and things of that nature.

Why does God only give the good things and not the bad things? Why is it that God has given you your longevity, but its not God that killed the person down the road who left three children orphaned?

Because God is a creation, not a destruction. God creates. God doesn't destroy. He created, and this is the fruit of his creation. That is what we are. We are very slow to recognise this. Well, anyway, this is my explanation to your question.

The Church has changed. In your lifetime, you have had Vatican II. You used to go to church in Latin, women weren't allowed on the altar and a priest didn't face the congregation.

Of course, the church has changed.

Do you think it needs to keep evolving, to keep changing?

(Sigh) Well, my simple contention is this: when talking about priests, chastity, and not getting married, I have said this before on a different occasion and now I say it publicly: if a priest wants to become a priest and only a priest, he should get married, but if a priest has aspirations to become a bishop or a cardinal then he should not get married. His responsibility will be beyond his family. He has to embrace everybody. The ordinary parish priest with a congregation that he has to care for, I would say that if he was married, then perhaps it would be an advantage for the congregation, because he would get a taste of what it is like to raise a family.

This is my contemplation on that score.

About the Catholic Church's evolution, I would say that it is necessary because we are going back to education programs. Everything used to be done in Latin, religions sprung from the latter, and they really tried to keep it in Latin, to keep the values of the religion, not to have it misinterpreted. Well now, what has happened is that it was necessary to depart from Latin and every nation adopted its own language. This is alright, providing the principles are maintained and not to conform with the wishes of the people. With some interpretations of the teaching, people formed different branches of religion, but they are still Christians. These are separations such as Jehovah's Witness, Seventh-day Adventist etc., they all sprung from the same religion.

For instance, I know a fellow who is not a Catholic and, on one occasion, we got into a discussion about religion.

This man that I was talking to, he asks, "Why should we have a church?" I replied, "How many monuments have we got in this world in recognition of great people? Heaps. Why shouldn't we have one for God, a church, or a temple? How many temples of the Buddhist do we have?"

Everybody always wants to glorify their Supreme being.

There are so many things that when you reach a certain age, the contradictions present themselves. And they seem to be justified. But I ask you, are they? Go deeper! And you will find the answer, if you want to, but if you choose not to, then it is easier, isn't it?

Through your life, have you ever wanted to find out more about another religion?

Well, I must say that I have never made it a business to find out about another religion, but I have observed and listened to other religions; I don't think that they are better than the one I have. They are not any better because I believe I got the right one to start with.

That is the Christian religion?

Yes.

What about Buddhism? It is a beautiful religion.

Buddhism is a beautiful religion, how right you are. I remember reading in a manuscript about a Buddhist monk who had the task to travel a certain distance. The distance and the path that he had to travel was considered impossible, but it was possible for him to undertake because of his faith. They described where he was and I am very sorry that I cannot recall the area, but it is in the Himalayas somewhere, and he managed to conquer and achieve because of his faith. He took the faith, and he achieved what was considered absolutely impossible. That is something that I can admire a lot. His faith was strong, and he was able to do things that others regarded as impossible!

What do you enjoy most about being a Christian?

Well, first and foremost, I enjoy my religion because I have proof that it helps me. I have been in difficult moments during my life and as a young man, I have been tempted to do the wrong thing. With another person, particularly with females, the temptation was there, but because of my religion and my belief, I didn't do it. I maintained myself and that is something that today, I treasure. For instance, I was saying to myself when I was young, why should I do this if I expect to find a girl who is a virgin? Follow what I mean? If I'm not myself, why should I expect it? I remember going to confession and the priest knew the family, Spinelli. He knew Maria[27], Rina, and their parents and Peter. He said to me, "I believe you are keeping company with Rina Spinelli?"

"Yes," I said, "I am."

"Well, treat her as your sister. She deserves it."

See, why should I remember this? It is coming from a priest.

I thought that was great, and I did treat her as a sister, in one aspect, you know. In spite of the desires, I had as a human, and no doubt she had hers, we accomplished that. I think that is what I mean about values and valuing things. These things, there are poems, there are songs, everything the human intellect owns has been used to describe the beauty of love. So, what I mean to say is we have got it, we are born with it — that ability to love. So why abuse it? Why not cherish it?

---

[27] Maria and Peter are Rina's siblings.

Let's get into your politics. Nonno, for us to have this conversation, you have to stay over there, and I have to say over here. (laughs). Okay?

We touched on it before, but I want to just recap and ask you, what nationality do you consider yourself to be?

Well, my nationality today is Australian, but my birth of right is Italy. I love Italy but I could not go against Australia; I could never do that.

We have talked about that story of when you were interned, when the captain asked you where your allegiance lies. I think that story challenges your sense of nationality to a degree that most people will never experience.

If you had to describe yourself in terms of political ideologies, where do you sit? Are you a socialist, nationalist, right wing? What do you believe?

First of all, I believe in democracy. It doesn't matter what party is in power; it has to be a democratic party. When you deviate from that, you are not fit to govern, in my view. In my early days in Australia, I thought the Labor Party was the party for the country because of what knowledge I had acquired and from what I could see. I thought the Labor Party was there for the poor, there for labourers, for the workers.

Throughout the years, I have found out that Labor fell down on the job. They had their values in their words, but not in practice. They weren't there for the worker. Under the Labor Party, there were groups that became independent of the government but were still supported by the government (unions). I didn't think that was fair in a democratic country. Why should anyone be imposed upon to belong to a union? Why should it be? It should be voluntary.

I do believe in unions, but it should be voluntary, and not imposed. You shouldn't have to be working on a job and have to belong to the union. Why should that union be a force in politics separate from the voted-in government? That is my argument.

We have a government elected by the people and it should govern. If it doesn't do the right thing, we should pull them out.

What about the compulsory voting in our democracy? Do you believe in that?

Well, in a democracy, compulsory voting, in a sense, is the right thing to do because everyone, as citizens, should have the knowledge to see what they want and what they don't like, and they should express that. If you are left to your own devices, to your own contemplation, you could really become a dictator yourself—and say, I'm not voting for anybody, I abstain from voting.

What are you doing then? You are doing that because you want to impose your own will, and you don't see any value in anybody that wants to be voted in. To come to that point, you really have to be knowledgeable about what you are doing and what is going on.

Yes, in a democracy, as a citizen, everyone has the right to vote, but when you are forcing people to vote, is it still a democracy?

Very true. Very true, why should it be necessary to force people to vote?

Why do you think that is different from voluntary union membership?

No, that is a different thing. It is different in this way — you are voting for a group. You form a group, and that group becomes a force, and it could influence the government, to the detriment of the rest of the citizens. And that group, the unions, are not voted in by the society.

So, you are saying that compulsory voting in democracy means you get a government elected. However, if you join a union, then this union can influence the government who is voted in and therefore impact everyone else?

That's right! They are there for themselves. I feel that unionism is necessary because where you work, you should make a group where you are united to ensure the right thing is done to the workers. We must work together to achieve, to improve, and to promote. That is why I think the union is necessary. But when you are forced to belong to a union, and then due to the numbers it has, the union is a political force; it is like having another political party — but one not elected by the whole of the people.

I have experiences in this. I knew men, friends of mine, who used to go downtown to collect their wages, without putting in a day's work, and the unions protected them. They were in the railways and in the ports, five or six of them. They never managed to work.

"Where are you going today?" I'd ask. "Oh, I've got to go and put in an appearance," they said, and this was to justify the wages.

Come on?! Hey! What about the man on a dole with a family? That makes me sick to think that a government would tolerate a group like that. When I was talking about the good Labor Party, we had a Prime Minister, Mr Chifley. He got the army down to the wharves, and he was a Labor man. Why? Because they were on strike, and they wouldn't work because they wanted higher wages. They wanted this and that, and it was too much to compete with the rest of the world. We couldn't send the merchandise overseas because it was too expensive; other countries wouldn't buy it from us. They all went on strike, and they got what they wanted in spite of everyone else. Hey! I mean to say, please!

I think you are saying ... think bigger than yourselves?

Of course, thinking universally is essential. If you love your country, you think of your neighbour, you think of the next person, you think of everybody, don't you? You don't create something of your own despite everyone else.

You see, today, in the ports, Australia is a thriving nation, and you cannot buy without selling or sell without buying. You have to trade, and this requires businesses to be rational and reasonable. You can't buy for ten and expect to sell for double the price because you are Australian. No, it doesn't work that way.

Today, there are wage increases. Where there are profits, why not increase the wages? But where there is the country that comes between the advantages and disadvantages, well, you have to make a choice and seek a middle way; you can't insist in spite of everything and everyone else.

Plato said the income of the highest paid in society should never amount to more than five times that of the lowest paid. Do you believe in an idea of capping how much people can earn?

I think capping earnings is a good idea. The point is that high wages come about because there is no competition for that position, so they are in demand and can charge a high amount. You see, that is where education comes in. Now you are educated, you have gone through university, you have learnt something, and you are entitled to a certain wage. The ones that didn't go through university, unfortunately, they are going to be subjected to that (educated) person, more or less. In certain ways, of course, no one is going to be forced to be subjected, but why didn't he study too?

He may not have had the means to do so, but he might not have had the will either. So, you find that in society, there is the one that wants and the other one that doesn't want to. If you don't seek to do anything, are you satisfied with your wage? Well, what can you do? This is a human element; it works that way.

But sometimes, people either don't have the will, or they can't. But there are also different types of people. Are you saying that because a certain job doesn't require a university degree that those people should be paid less?

I can support that by saying this, if he is in a position to get a thousand dollars a week more than another fellow, it is because he has the brains to create the work for this fellow. Follow what I mean? You see, that is what we need in this world. And we have to accept this. We have got the man that provides the work and there is a man that does the work. The one that provides the work he has to have brains; he has to have ability, to create industry to be able to employ people. Now, why shouldn't we recognise the working man who works and gets his wages, so why shouldn't we also recognise the value of the boss, and therefore, the higher wage?

The thing is this: what is wrong is totally different from what we are talking about. The working man, in a well-established factory, should be given the opportunity to have shares in the factory. Follow what I mean? To recognise the man ahead, respect him. It is like children respecting their father; he is providing for them, so why don't you respect him?

This is what I believe: the man that works should be given the opportunity to be part and parcel of the success of the business. He should have a percentage of the total income. Separate from their income. He should be able to say, "I am working for you all right, but at the end of the year, on top of my wages, I want a dividend."

We should recognise and be recognised by the man that gives work and employs men, instead of making bloomin' slaves of them. You work this or you get the sack, you know?! Give a man a chance to be part and parcel of the whole process.

That is where the union can come in, can't it?

Exactly, that is the value of a union.

Because a union can stop the employer from exploiting his or her employees.

Well, we are going back to the principles, the morals and the Ten Commandments! You should not abuse the next person.

So, you are talking about the responsibility that comes with power?

The responsibility that comes with intelligence, with adaptation, when you are intelligent and you work, then you adapt, and you inspire.

When I became President of the Club Marconi, what did I do there? I could detail different episodes.

The things that I encountered were many. I met a fellow down at the Club on Sunday, and he came over and shook hands with me and said, "I'll never forget you." He continued, "You spent fifteen minutes with me and what you said saved my life." I talked to him, and I convinced him that what he was doing was the wrong thing. After all these years! It must be about twenty years ago since this happened.

You see, the teaching of our religion, the teaching of Christ and the Ten Commandments, these are all the basis of civilisation. You know who said this? It was President Ronald Reagan of the USA. He said, "If only all of us complied with the Ten Commandments, we wouldn't be having any war, we would be living like brothers and sisters; we would be equals."

Why shouldn't I be considered as a human, instead of getting exploited? We get bills from the telephone company and from the bank; they enclose an envelope with a form for you to fill in to pay by post instead of going to the bank. Oh, come on!

They charge you to go to the bank, to deal over the counter now.

They better not charge that to me when I go into the bank! I'll tell you what! I will ring up the bank manager. (Oh Felicity, the things that become a process, it is not funny).

Okay, okay, did you see the list of the names of the Socceroos?

That is what I said to Mr David Hill, the Chairman of Soccer Australia. When he went to Club Marconi, he wanted to abolish all names of soccer clubs that referred to a nationality and one thing or another. You know what I said to him? He recorded it and I said, *"Tell Mr Hill that we are more Australian than he will ever be. The Soccer Clubs represent Australia, they are all ethnic, from ethnic backgrounds, and proudly, they sing the Australian Anthem."*

CHAPTER EIGHT
Life

*"If you don't love, you don't tolerate.
If you don't love, you make yourself righteous and
you don't consider the feelings of the next person."*

In your life, you have assumed many leadership roles within the Club and church. What do you think are the qualities of a good leader?

I would say to be a good leader, you must have integrity. You must be honest, and you must consider others if you expect others to consider you. You must also be a good (social) mixer, and you must be equipped with a lot of tolerance. If you have all of these qualities, then you stand a good chance of being appreciated by the people you mix with and are able to be a good leader of people.

What do you believe are the most important qualities that a person should have?

I could add this much to what I have already; it is important to have extended values in the community as a married man and as a father. First of all, as a good husband and as a father, then being ready to accept and give help when it is needed — to be charitable and be grateful with everything you do.

What do you think people should be striving toward in their lives personally, and what do you think society should be striving for?

Well, in a sense, we have already discussed this when talking about values and family life.

Only as recently as yesterday, I had the occasion to get into this discussion.

In order to have sound politics and sound politicians, we would not stand a chance if they did not come from a good family. If we go back and analyse the best politicians we have ever had, they have had good relations with their parents. They were family people; they loved their parents, their brothers and sisters, and they strove to be helpful in society.

Now, if we depart from those principles, I'm afraid we wouldn't stand a chance to have anything decent in society.

So, you very much see the individual as an important part of a wider society because of the effects of their life on society?

Yes, exactly, the individual is an important part of a wider society.

I want you to answer this question as if you are talking to your grandchildren and great grandchildren. You have been married for a very long time, fifty-eight years, in fact. What are the ingredients to a long and successful marriage?

It is a very appropriate question, and I hope I will be able to give you the right answer. To give you the right answer, I can only relate to my partner and myself. The fact is, first of all, there is love. Without that, you wouldn't accomplish anything. If you don't love, you don't tolerate. If you don't love, you make yourself righteous and you don't consider the feelings of the next person.

All of these qualities have to be embraced by a couple, by each other.

I was once told by an independent person, an elderly man, when he knew I was keeping company with my wife, he said: "Remember never to quarrel at the same time. When an argument takes place, listen until the opposition is finished, and then you talk. Don't try and ram things down their throat. Wait until your partner is finished and your partner waits for you to finish." I think that was good advice.

It is great advice; so simple yet true.

Yes, it was simple and classic. That is something I have tried to apply. I can't deny the fact that sometimes we get into arguments over different things. But we have never not spoken to each other for more than a couple of hours. We understand and forgive and feel there are times and moments when we don't feel well physically, or something is irritating us, and one can react out of this. These are things that a couple must reason and say to themselves, *I wonder why they said this or that?* When you stop and think, you find the solution and when you find the solution, it's okay. That goes with being honest with each other. I'm sometimes wondering that maybe there is something wrong with Rina, but how am I supposed to know unless she says something.

That's a point. When Rina is not feeling well, she clams up. She doesn't talk or say anything. I learnt, after many times, to ask, "What is the matter?" Of course I get an answer, maybe not voluntarily, and probably because she doesn't want to tell me that she doesn't feel well, but I do get an answer, and we seek a remedy.

This next question is about getting to know you as a person, Nonno, not by what you have done, but rather why.

What were the most important things to you when you left Italy, compared to when you were thirty-five, compared to now?

I left Italy with the objective to go back in three years. It was the Depression, and the misery that I thought I left in Italy, I found in Australia. Unemployment was dreadful. It is not like the Depression of today. It is not to be compared to the 1930s, before World War 2.

Anyway, I came here. We struggled and saved, and the idea was to bring the rest of the family to Australia. There was a time that my father was considering going back to Italy, but he could not leave me here on my own. That is how we came to buy the little property in Smithfield and, of course, we had to go into debt to buy the property and I always contributed to the debt we had. This all went to benefit the whole family.

The most important thing then was the family?

Yes, family is so important — my parents and my brothers being together.

So, what was important to you when you were thirty-five years old?

I was married with children when I was thirty-five. From early 1934, when I left my employment and joined my father, we worked together as market gardeners. We produced, we saved, and we persevered. We bought more properties and finished up with many acres of land in different places.

The idea was my father would give each one of us a block of land to start off our married life. We never had a chance to learn a trade. First of all, there was the language barrier, and secondly, there was no work. So, we had to do our best to become self-sufficient, independent, work for ourselves, and perhaps, help others. That's how things were at that time.

The time came that I got myself a truck to bring my own produce to the market, and I found that my brothers and my cousins wanted to give me stuff to sell. I finished up with about twenty customers, so I never had time to grow anything. I leased my land to a friend of mine to work on (in shares) and I would sell the produce.

I used to operate at the market and what I would sell for others was on a commission basis.

Did you enjoy working in the markets as a break from the physical labour?

I was independent, and I used to do my own work when selling to the markets, so I found satisfaction in making all of these people happy, those I cared for like my brothers. I got a lot of satisfaction because occasionally, they would invite us to dinner to show their gratitude.

Then, I decided that I had had enough of that because it meant getting up at 3 am to 4 am and struggling down at the markets, selecting all the stuff. It was hard work jumping up and down from the truck for this and that and the stuff and keeping the books for the sales.

It was a busy time and returning home in the truck, I always wanted to sleep. On one occasion, I found myself driving on the wrong side of the road. Lucky there was no on-coming traffic.

What truck was that?

The Chevrolet, although I finished going to the markets with the Ford. The big green Ford.

Arthur used to come with me in the Ford. Then, he was offered a job managing another company, and he worked for them, so I was left on my own. I borrowed your other grandfather, Andrew Agius, to help me. He would come to my place in the morning, and I would take him to the markets to help me prepare things and serve customers. We were real pals. I would pay him, of course.

Anyway, we got on well and I trusted him. I would leave him to look after the business and when I came back, he had sold things and collected money.

So, what are the most important things to you now?

Well, once I left the markets, I was offered a job in real estate. I was in real estate for a number of years buying and selling and I worked for Fornasier Real Estate at Canley Vale.

Did you like it?

I can't say I liked it a lot because sometimes we weren't busy. I had an office and sometimes, I had to just sit around.

How much did you sell homes for then?

Oh, $15,000 to $20,000 was an average sales price for a house. It depended.

Now, I find myself down at Stocklands, Wetherill Park, and someone says to me, "Don't you remember me? You sold me a place."

I was in the real estate business for three years.

What is important now?

Well, leaving finances aside, the most important thing of all is that our children are happily married and doing well. All have their families which are beautiful and healthy. Now we are getting great-grandchildren, and my hope is that I see most of them, and most importantly, that everyone is happy and prosperous. We live for their happiness and progress.

What do you believe are your finest achievements and the proudest moments in life?

My life has been a multitude of events that make me what I am, happy and contented.

The only thing I find against my will and body is my health. I find myself with a young mind and an old body. There are things around that I would love to do, but I'm dependent. That dependency really bothers and worries me, as I feel I should be able to cope by myself. I was told that I expect too much and have to realise my age and look around and see what others do. I do that, but there are people around older than me that do better than I.

On the other hand, there are not many around that are my age, so I am thankful. Summing everything up, I have every right to thank God. Thank him for providing for everything I have, my wife, children, grandchildren, and everything. We are very, very fortunate, and lucky.

If you skim through all of your life and experiences and come up with a piece of advice for your children, grandchildren, and young people, what advice would you give?

One thing, above all, is to be loveable. If you succeed at being loveable, it means you are a contented person. Appreciate who you are and what you've got, appreciate the road you've taken and are travelling on. In other words, your happiness is my happiness and Rina's.

We are not here for wealth, comfort, or luxury. I feel that luxury is for our offspring, grandchildren, and great grandchildren. We would only be content to see everyone happy and healthy. BEAUTIFUL!

We talked about when you left Italy, your ambition was to return after three years. When you eventually went back, forty years later, what were you feeling?

I was full of expectations. Thank God my expectations weren't exorbitant, but normal expectations that any human being could wish for. Meeting my school friends, my town, and the people ... I felt reborn. Going back after forty years, speaking my own language, conversing about things I knew and grew up with, I felt like I was reborn. I thought, *This is living.* It was great.

I had a schoolmate who became the headmaster at the elementary school in town. It was Sunday, so I looked for him and I was told he was at the school. The school had long corridors with classrooms on one side facing north and the corridor was under cover because of the weather in Italy.

I could hear someone shuffling in one of the classes, so I called out, "Quido Chilani?" He came out and just stood there. He didn't recognise me. After forty years, we didn't look the same. I said, "Hello Quido."

He said, "Who are you?"

I said, "It's me, Felice."

When I told him who I was, we just fell into each other's arms. What a moment and experience. If I live 1,000 years, I will never forget it.

When we departed, I went to see him at his home with his family and wife. Again, we embraced, and we both cried. When I went back again, I went to see him, and we didn't have the emotional stuff we went through the last time. No, I said, I could do without that. In *Sesto*, I recorded people's messages and the mass that was celebrated, as well as the bells.

The first time I went to Italy, we landed in Rome, and took a flight to Venice, and then a bus to the town of *Portogruaro*. To me, things seemed to have diminished, and things had obviously changed when we arrived in town. My uncle and aunty (my mother's sisters) were at church. Another family lived further away, and a girl came out, Rosina. Her grandmother was my father's aunty- my grandfather's sister.

Despite the changes, we had a wonderful time there. We went to dinner at the local restaurant, and we had a party with everyone.

How long were you there?

We were there for three months. We hired a car and went back to Rome through all the big towns and cities such as Assissi, Milan, Piacenza (where Rina's family is from), Turin, and Florence, all of these places. Sometimes, we drove on the wrong side of the road! From there, we went to Spain and France.

You have come from very humble beginnings, and when you came to Australia, it was hard work. What was it like for you to be the tourist somewhere and step out of the working life for a change? To go travel and see the world?

The answer to this can be explained in many ways. To give the right emphasis, you've got to be a bit conversive with the world at large. I always kept myself informed of the events of the world and the nature of different countries because, here in Australia, you continue to mix with French, German, Spanish, Greek, and people of all cultures.

You already have a sort of expectation of what you'll find. In fact, on the first trip, we landed in Athens, Greece. We didn't understand a word of the Greek language. I found it very odd that they use a lot of the letters we use, but place them in such a way that we could not pronounce them. We would go for a walk, and we would say to each other, "We better remember where we are because we don't know the name of the streets." We couldn't read them!

In Athens, we went to see the ancient arenas, the ancient Acropolis—all the columns and the amphitheatre.

But what was it like? You've left Italy at fifteen years old, and you had only been in Australia.

Just as well I was conversant, and I read up on the history of this and that. Just as well, otherwise it would have been like coming out of the grave.

I was very happy and grateful for the opportunity to travel. The Italian Government gave me a free trip to Italy because I was a good citizen and a good Italian in Australia.

Was this when you were made a *Cavaliere*?

Yes, a *Cavaliere* is a knight of the Italian Republic.

How did that occur?

With my activities in Smithfield at the church, we used to have dances there. I organised these with a committee, a wonderful group of young men. We used to have fiestas and dances to raise money for the church. After that I got involved with the Club. I became President of the Club and, as president, I had the occasion to meet the Italian Consulate which I had met before with other dignitaries. I extended the friendship to Blacktown Workers Club, Smithfield RSL, Cabra-Vale RSL, and other clubs around. We used to invite other clubs to functions, and I used to go to their clubs. So, I did a lot of community work that got me noticed.

Were you nominated?

Yes, someone suggested my name for an award to the Italian authorities when the President of Italy, Mr Saraga, came to Australia. I was President of Club Marconi then. He wasn't here for long, and he didn't come to the Club. He met all the Italians at Town Hall, Sydney, and I met him and had dinner on the Italian ship that brought him here.

Gough Whitlam was there as well as the dignitaries of the time, including the Prime Minister of the time, Harold Holt. They went to see the Fiat Factory at Homebush, where the trucks and cars from Italy come to. I was very despondent that day because Rina was in hospital getting her gallstones removed and she wasn't very well when I went to see her.

This man, Mr Saraga, made me a *Cavaliere*, and the Italian Consulate presented me with the medal.

You came here at fifteen years old. How has the language barrier been for you? How has it prohibited you?

Well, the Italian language, like the English language, has progressed with time. Some of the words and pronunciation of phrases weren't around, even in my day, when I was at school. Even in *La Fiamma*, I need the dictionary to know what they mean. [28] I work it out by putting two and two together, of course.

Is it often that you don't understand what is written?

When they talk about politics or sport in *La Fiamma*, the expressions they use are sometimes different from my time. I speak the 'old Italian' of my days.

When you speak Italian, are you speaking the *Sesto* dialect or proper Italian?

The Italian I speak depends on who I meet and speak with. I prefer to speak proper Italian because it is easier than my other language/dialect.

Is that what you learned at school and the dialect you learned at home?

Yes, that is right, and they are different.

With the English-Australian language, you can just imagine how difficult that is when I am unable to express myself or ask and say things. I think I narrated to you the experience I had when I was first given a horse to ride and had to muster some cows and about the goanna?

Yes! You thought it was a crocodile!

I couldn't say anything but *cocodrillo*!!

---

[28] *La Fiamma* is an Italian-language Australian newspaper.

So, the language has been a burden to you?

Yes, it was difficult. Just as well that I knew a terrific lady, Mrs Noble. She would go out of her way to explain things to me. She was very patient. She was like a mother to me. I used to cook for myself. I was fifteen or sixteen years old, and I used to do my own cooking, and washing clothes, and mending.

The other day, I was talking about the modern way of living with Rina, and she says they don't put patches on things these days. I used to put patches on my pants' knees and socks; anything to save money.

How do you feel about your health problems as you are so active mentally?

Dependency is the most difficult thing, at my age. The only comfort I have is Rina and my daughters, in particular, who are close to us. Our sons, we don't expect because they have their own families.

We do understand and appreciate that fully, but what bothers me is that I do need the help of my sons occasionally, and I know they have their own commitments with family, and that comes first. I understand because my family came first too. So, it is only fair I accept that fully.

It hurts me to ask them. For instance, Arthur was talking about getting some wood, one Saturday, and we went to the place where I also get the wood from, one trailer load, at a time. I didn't need any, at the time, but when I did, I had to ring Arthur and ask him to help. I didn't want to because he only has one day to do things at home.

I ended up getting it delivered, and they dumped it in front of the shed and that was no good because I couldn't stack it away. So, I still needed help. So, you see, you become dependent. I can't ask Joe because, even on a Sunday, he is at the factory. It would only be natural for Arthur to ask why I didn't seek Joe's help, but I couldn't.

We used to have Adam come around and cut the grass before he got married, and he used to do a lot of things for me. Now when he comes around, he asks if he can do anything, and I appreciate that very much.

What does it do to Felice Zadro when he can't 'pick up the wood'?

Actions that show my age depresses me and that is why I said I have a young head in an old body. I get frustrated because I can see things that need to be done but cannot do them as easily ... or at all.

How do you deal with that?

I have to sit back and think of how old I am and how much I have achieved and be grateful and content. People say to me: "What do you expect at your age? You're wonderful; you're this and that, be happy." It's not easy.

We have been talking with each other for months now Nonno about a lot of issues, times and your memories from your lifetime. I would like to thank you for sharing your story with me.

We have laughed, I've had tears, and you have amazed me with your experiences, resilience and determination. I am honoured to be your granddaughter, not only for your achievements, but for the person that you are.

Is there anything else you would like to say that we haven't talked about Nonno?

I was lucky to have a granddaughter, Felicity, who has taken the trouble to listen to my narration, and about what I had to say in my old age and about my life.

I thank her very much.

PHOTOS

Felice Zadro circa, 1938.

Rina Spinelli, Miss Fairfield.

Rina Spinelli, making her debutante.

Wedding Day, 1939
Left to right David Zadro, Gloria Becchio, Felice Zadro,
Rina Zadro, Jack Bazzano.

Felice and Rina.

Family members - Felice and Rina centre.

(Back row) Felice, Rina
(L-R Pauline, Maria, Joseph and Arthur).

The Old House at 105 Bossley Park Road, Bossley Park.
A new house was built on this location.

Back row (L-R) Joseph and Esterina Zadro, Bruno and
Pauline Viler, Maria and Victor Gobbo (holding Natalie Gobbo)
Caroline and Arthur Zadro, Rina (holding Loretta Zadro nee
McPherson) and Felice Zadro.
Front row (L-R) Adrian Zadro, Maria Zadro (Felice's mother),
Mark Viler and Peter Viler (pram).

Felice and Rina, circa 60s.

Felice Zadro, Gough Whitlam Prime Minister of Australia, Rina Zadro (man unknown). Taken at Club Marconi.

Back row (L-R)
Arthur Zadro,
Maria Gobbo,
Pauline Viler,
Joseph Zadro.
Front row (L-R)
Rina and Felice Zadro

Back row (L-R) Angela Santelmann, Caroline Zadro.
Mid row (L-R) Natalie Gobbo, Maria Gobbo, Felice (as Santa)
Pauline Viler, Loretta McPherson
Next row (L-R) Rina Zadro, Catherine Delnawaz, Helena
Zadro-Jones (on lap), Paris Delnawaz (hidden), Felicity Zadro
Front row (L-R) Angela Zadro-Jones, Veronica Viler,
Elizabeth Zadro.

Rina and Felice at a Ball at Club Marconi.

Ian Thorley, Gough Whitlam and Felice Zadro, 1964.

Felice and Rina, 50th Wedding annivesary.

Family picnic, 2002.

Felice and Rina at their home in Bossley Park.

Rina and Felice Zadro, pioneer Italian migrants of the Fairfield district.

From the Fairfield City Heritage Collection, Felice and Rina Zadro.

Valentine's day.

Fairfield International Monument.

Fairfield International Monument.

Fairfield International Monument.

ARTICLES

The following pages contain a sample of newspaper clippings that Rina had kept in her papers for years. Any handwriting seen on the clippings is Rina's.

> born.
> Here is news of a very fine public gesture which should be appreciated by the entire population of the district. On Sunday last Mr. Felix Zadro called on the president of Smithfield Ward Hospital Committee, and notified him that the Italian community felt it their duty to do their bit towards helping the hospital appeal. They had already commenced organising one of their always well patronised dances, to be held at St. Gertrude's Hall on Saturday, August 14 (proceeds to Miss Cecill Walker's candidature). Yes, we agree — a fine gesture, indeed.

1954 article

13 Oxford Street,

SMITHFIELD.

11th September, 1954.

Mr. P. Zadro,
Oxford Street,
SMITHFIELD.

Dear Mr. Zadro,

On behalf of the District Hospital Appeal (Smithfield Ward Committee) I extend to your Committee and all who assisted in making a recent Dance in aid of Miss Cecily Walker's Queen Candidature, such an outstanding success, our sincere thanks and appreciation. I feel that the thoughtful consideration shown on the part of the Italian Community is something which you are all entitled to be proud of and one which has earnt you all the respect of the entire community. Added to the thanks of my Committee, is my personal thanks and congratulations on the most thorough organising it has been my good fortune to witness during my long association with public life in this district.

Again thanking you and wishing your Committee a most successful future.

Yours truly,

R. J. H. McLeod

PRESIDENT.

SMITHFIELD WARD HOSPITAL APPEAL COMMITTEE.

19th October 1967

SETTEGIORNI

NOTIZIE DI CRONACA

ELEZIONI CLUB MARCONI

FELICE ZADRO
riconfermato Presidente

All'assemblea dei soci, tenutasi domenica scorsa, abbiamo avuto la chiara dimostrazione della bella vitalità del sodalizio di Bossley Park e del buon senso di coloro che ne fanno parte.

Non sono mancati gli interventi, le mozioni e qualche breve ma contenuto dibattito. Tutte cose che stanno a dimostrare quanto grande sia l'interesse dei soci per la vita e lo sviluppo del Club.

La riconferma di Felice Zadro a Presidente, avvenuta con largo margine di voti, oltre che meritata è anche significativa. La maggioranza dei votanti ha inteso cioè ridare pieno mandato a un uomo che ha voluto e saputo elevarsi al disopra degli interessi di gruppi e di singoli.

Il Club Marconi è e deve essere il Club di tutti gli italiani, senza distinzioni di sorta. La sua funzione ricreativa, sportiva e sociale mira ad u-na sempre migliore intesa con gli australiani e serve alla causa di una sana assimilazione in questa nostra terra di adozione.

Questo è il credo del Presidente Felice Zadro, il quale merita l'appellativo di Presidente della **Unione della Comunità Italiana**.

Non possiamo che congratularci per la scelta fatta dalla assemblea.

Auguri e buon lavoro ai membri vecchi e nuovi dell'italianissimo Club Marconi.

La nuova composizione del direttivo del club è la seguente:

Presidente: Felice Zadro; v.presidenti: A. Bagatella, C. Mariani; membri: V. Budini, G. Calabro', G. Castellano, G. Cessario, R. Dalla Vecchia, L. Marson, R. Mileto, G. Morizzi, P. Perotto.

21 October 1967

Assemblea ed elezioni al Club Marconi

Felice Zadro rieletto presidente

Bossley Park, 18 ottobre

DOMENICA scorsa, alla presenza di una folla record di soci (446 per la cronaca) si è svolta l'assemblea generale del Club Marconi con la elezione del nuovo comitato direttivo.

Il rapporto del presidente F. Zadro ed il rapporto finanziario sono stati approvati senza obiezione alcuna. Del resto i traguardi raggiunti dal comitato in carica negli ultimi dodici mesi non offriva spunto a critiche valevoli e gli interlocutori che si sono alzati a parlare non hanno avuto che espressioni di lode ed ammirazione per la mole di lavoro svolto, per le iniziative che hanno fatto onore al club e aperto alla comunità italiana la strada a manifestazioni regionali una migliore dell'altra.

Il profitto netto di $38 mila 645.17 con i suoi $12 mila 658 in più dell'annata precedente, testimonia il successo della suddetta attività.

Il valore patrimoniale del Club è salito da $396.080 a $413.423. Il numero dei membri del Club è salito a 1930.

Presidente e segretario (L. Benedetti) hanno avuto parole di alto elogio per il comitato femminile di cui è presidente la signora Crosio.

Si sono infine svolte le elezioni che hanno dato il seguente risultato: presidente: Felice Zadro (rieletto a grandissima maggioranza); vicepresidenti: A. Bagatella e C. Mariani; consiglieri: V. Budini, G. Calabrò, G. Castellano, G. Cessario, R. Dalla Vecchia, L. Marson, R. Mileto, G. Morizzi, P. Perrotto.

Fra le prossime attività del Club ricordiamo il picnic che avrà luogo il 22 ottobre ed il ballo del calcio che sarà tenuto la sera del 28 ottobre.

GUARANTEED CIRCULATION 28,000 COPIES

Chronicle
FAIRFIELD - CABRAMATTA

THE SYLVIA BEAUTY SALON
Exclusive Hair Styling
5 THE MALL, WARE STREET
Phone FAIRFIELD 72-5908
PERMS ... FROM $5.50
We also specialise in
WIGS AND HAIRPIECES
OPEN ALL DAY WEDNESDAY
& THURSDAY NIGHT TILL 9 p.m.

Richard Britton
REAL ESTATE
6 SPENCER ST., FAIRFIELD
(Opposite Council Chambers)
PHONE 72-2955 (Office Hours)

Delivered free throughout the Fairfield-Cabramatta Municipality including Bonnyrigg, Bossley Park, Canley Vale, Carramar, Chester Hill, Fairfield Heights, Horsley Park, Lansvale, Mt. Pritchard, Smithfield, Villawood, Yennora.

OFFICE: THE CRESCENT, FAIRFIELD (Next to Crescent Theatre). PHONE: 72-5833 or 602-8216

VOL. 15, No. 38   TUESDAY, OCTOBER 1, 1968   Registered under the Newspaper Act. 1898

1968

Cook voyage celebrated

ITALIAN CLUB GIVES A LEAD IN PATRIOTISM

The large, hospitable Club Marconi at Bossley Park excelled itself last Saturday night with a memorable and imaginative social function—its second annual "Australian Night".

The function was not wholly, as one might imagine, designed to "Australianise" new - Australian Italians and to help assimilate them into "the Australian way of life."

It was to extend the hand of friendship to Australian friends of the Club Marconi members and more important, to illustrate the historic tradition of Australia, and to give old and new Australians alike a greater interest in that tradition.

Club foundation

The club decided that its second "Australian Night" should commemorate the 200th anniversary of the departure of Captain James Cook from England in 1768 on "his voyage of discovery in Australia".

The evening also celebrated the 10th anniversary of the foundation of the Club Marconi.

As the guests arrived they were greeted by young people dressed in the colourful costumes of the 17th century.

These young people later danced the graceful Minuet to give the audience an idea of the chivalry and splendour of that age.

The dancers (all pupils of Roy Viletta's ballet school at Bankstown) were Roy Viletta, Chris Miller, Annette Devereaux, Annette Smith, Robert Chard, Joseph Millward.

Aborigine sings

But the true Australian flavour of the night was imparted by the engagement of popular aboriginal singer Jimmy Little, as guest artist and four aborigines — descendants of early tribes — to support him.

The four aborigines, in corroboree make-up, played their didgeridoes and music sticks and chanted corroboree songs on stage and later "accompanied" Jimmy as he sang.

The walls of the club were brightly decorated with Australian and Italian flags and "Waltzing Matilda" was prominent among the Australian songs presented.

Guests of club

Among the official guests of the club welcomed by Club President (Mr. P. Zadro) were Ald. K. Makepeace (representing the Mayor, Ald. H. Schofield) and Ald. Thorley, of Fairfield Council; Mr. Arthur West, President of Cabra Vale Ex-Servicemen's Club; Mr. P. J. Johnsson, President of Fairfield R.S.L. Club; Mr. Walsh, of Blacktown Workers' Club; Dr. E. Liotta, Commercial Attache of the Italian Embassy; Dr. S. Bini, representing the Italian Consul-General; Mr. A. Cleaver (Chronicle newspaper) wives; Mr. B. Carroll, Field Officer of the Foundation for Aboriginal Affairs; and Mr. Fowler, of the Nepean River Historical Museum, and their wives.

History display

The stage decoration was an historical display in itself comprising aboriginal and tribal weapons, a set of miner's gear from the Eureka Stockade days, three early Miner's Rights, a manual vacuum cleaner of 1890, and an ice cream machine of 1950 — plus a bell and chain.

The display was arranged by the Nepean River Valley Historical Museum.

Copies of the "London Gazette" of 1685 reporting on Captain Cook's departure for "The Great South—
● CONTINUED PAGE 2.

Meeting on plan

Objections will be lodged by Bossley Park residents to the Fairfield Council's zoning plan for the Municipality as it adversely affects Bossley Park.

The Bossley Park Progress Association will be holding a special meeting at the Progress Hall, in Mimosa Road, on Wednesday, October 9 at 8 p.m.

All interested citizens are invited to attend and express their views on the zoning question.

The Association's President (Mr. Joe Palakaras) reminds Bossley Park residents that if they wish to lodge any objection to the Zoning Plan at present on exhibition at the Fairfield Council Chambers, they have only a few days more in which to act.

TAX RETURNS
AND ALL
Accounting Matters
A. C. EVETT
PHONE 72-4024

Distinctive Portraits

VICINNA STUDIOS
CRESCENT THEATRE,
FAIRFIELD • 72-5833

Homes Wanted
Buyers waiting for all types of Property.
Priced from $2,800 to $14,000.
REGAL ESTATE AGENCY

Burns
194 Cabram

WHITE WINGS
Cake M
19c

K.R. PICNIC SHOUL
1¼ lb.
$1.25
LABELS FROM THESE
FOR

THE MEN WITH A DREAM

Migrants plan a mini-university

By EDWIN LEANE

NEW SOUTH Wales is expected to be the proving ground for a bold, new experiment in migrant assimilation.

Spearheaded by Sydney's Italian community, the project is multi-national and multi-denominational.

It will take the form of an educational and cultural centre, land for which has been earmarked at Bossley Park, Fairfield.

The intention is to provide a place where children of migrants continue their studies in their own language, augmented by intensive tuition in English.

As soon as individual students are judged competent to continue their education in English, they will be streamed into the Australian school system.

Mr Armand Madaro, social secretary of the Marconi Club and a man intimately involved in the scheme, said this week: "The proposed centre will also be a haven for misplaced intellectuals from the old continent."

Professional people with European qualifications, will be able to retrain at the centre to acquire Australian documents of proficiency.

"This should eliminate the absurd situation we have at present where skilled doctors are working as nurses, or professors are employed as labourers," he said.

The centre has been under consideration for some time.

Events moved apace this week, however, after the visit of Archbishop Cunial, the apostolic delegate to migrant communities throughout the world.

An eminent cleric, Archbishop Cunial is better known to Roman Catholic congregations as Viceregent of Rome.

KEY ROLE

He was accompanied by Liberio Andreatta, of the Cavanis Fathers, a teaching order based in Venice.

If the scheme goes ahead, the Cavanis Fathers are expected to play a key role in the teaching procedures.

But Mr Madaro emphasised that 90 per cent of the complement would be lay staff — some from Italy and the others from Australia.

All nationalities and all religions would be catered for.

Archbishop Cunial has already pledged the Vatican's moral support for the educational and cultural centre, and will be reporting to the Pope on the financial aspects.

Expressions of support have also come from Mr Lorenzo Motz, the Italian vice-consul in Sydney, and Professor Giovanni Frasca, education adviser attached to the Italian Embassy in Canberra.

The result of talks with Federal ministers and the NSW Department of Education has not yet been announced.

Mr Felice Zadro, the Marconi Club president, said that if the Bossley Park project came to fruition, similar educational and cultural centres would be set up in Queensland and Victoria.

Mr Zadro came to Australia 44 years ago and appreciates, better than most, the problems of newly arrived migrants.

A sturdy, soft-spoken man held in high esteem by the Italian community, Mr Zadro becomes introspective when he recalls his early years in Australia.

"I had my sixteenth birthday here," he said. "You cannot believe how lonely I was.

"I used to walk to the top of a hill at sunset and strain my eyes to see as far as possible into the distance.

"I thought, just once, I might be able to see my beloved Italy."

Felice Zadro learned to adjust, and came to terms with his Australian neighbours.

But it was hard, and often heartbreaking.

Now he wants to make it easier for those following in his footsteps.

Cosimo Mariani and Angelo Bagatella, vice-president of the Marconi Club, also have stories of hardship and unhappiness to relate.

And they spoke last week of a disturbing new phenomenon — resentment among the younger generation towards their parents for being Italian.

"If children are ostracised at school by their fellow pupils, or downgraded in class because they simply don't understand their teacher, trouble soon follows," Mr Mariani said.

"They lose interest in their studies, learn to hate school, and become resentful and spiteful at home."

Mr Bagatella said: "There can be serious psychological repercussions.

"They see themselves as intellectual failures. Children can be very cruel."

If the educational and cultural centre is established at Bossley Park, the students will be fortunate indeed.

EXPELLED

The Marconi Club, within walking distance, will also satisfy their social and recreational needs.

It sprawls over 44 acres and provides an enormous range of activities for its members, not all of whom are Italian.

It takes its name from the Italian inventor, whose bust dominates the entrance lobby.

A feature of the club is the fine of bocce alley where members play their version of bowls.

Armand Madaro, its social secretary, is an intellectual with an artistic national reputation.

In 1967, he was appointed a Knight of the French Academy for his contributions to French culture.

Formerly, he taught languages at De Lesseps College in Cairo, to which he lost in the building of Suez Canal Company employees.

Mr Madaro was expelled, along with many other foreign nationals, when the canal was nationalised.

Mr Madaro (left) and Mr Zadro. The site of the proposed centre is the hillock on the far right.

Members of the Marconi Club playing bocce, a version of bowls.

LOOKING BEHIND THE NEWS

The living textbook

on Tuesday in
The Sydney Morning Herald

This week's topics:

✻ Newspapers in school: How to get the best out of them.
✻ 1973: Metrics touch our daily lives

Students learn more when they read
Looking Behind the News every week
It stays in front of the textbooks.
Have the Herald delivered to your home so that
your children can keep ahead in their class work.

The Sydney Morning Herald

The more you think about it, the more you need the Herald

Pag. 4 — 6 luglio 1973 — SETTEGIORNI

Presentate a Whitlam le debuttanti
MARCONI GALA BALL

Accumunata agli applausi per la Attard e per i giovani esecutori, l'orchestra di Ezio Gribaldi.
Le nove ragazze debuttanti: Josephine Del Giudice, Patricia Caretta, Gianna Raffaelli, Marteza Pisani-Rossi, Diana Rosetto, Laura Maghet, Doris Fresch, Lorraine Fontana, Barbara Vollar e i loro rispettivi cavalieri: Frank Mammolite, Livio Sartoretto, Roberto Zadro, Joe Luca, Damian Frassetto, Wally Maghet, Tony Zappa, Silvio Vagli, Adriano Morrone sono stati presentati al Primo Ministro e alla signora Whitlam.
In precedenza, il presidente del Club F. Zadro aveva dato il benvenuto alle personalità presenti. Whitlam, rispondendo, aveva avuto per la nostra comunità e per gli immigrati in genere, espressioni di simpatia.
Dopo la presentazione delle debuttanti, danze fino ad oltre la mezzanotte. Pubblico soddisfattissimo e lusinghieri commenti sulla riuscitissima serata, commenti

Club Marconi.
Il servizio fotografico che appare in questa pagina è stato eseguito dal popolare Eddie Camilleri titolare dello Studio Minerva.

Il Primo Ministro Whitlam e la consorte durante la presentazione delle debuttanti.

Da sinistra: il Primo Ministro Whitlam, la signora Whitlam, la signora Zadro, il presidente del Club Marconi F. Zadro e il segretario-direttore A. Frabboni.

SYDNEY — L'edizione 1973 del tradizionale Ballo annuale del Club Marconi e' riuscita splendidamente. Oltre 800 persone hanno affollato il grande salone delle feste del Club per questo eccezionale "Gala Ball" al quale quest'anno ha presenziato il Primo Ministro d'Australia Whitlam.
Fra gli ospiti d'onore, insieme a Whitlam e alla consorte, erano presenti il deputato federale on. Klugman e signora, il Senatore F. Calabro e il deputato Ferguson con le rispettive consorti, il Vice Console dr. Mott, il dr. Piccirilli della Ambasciata d'Italia, il Sindaco di Fairfield Turdle e signora e il Direttore del Dipartimento d'Immigrazione Waterman.
La sfilata e la presentazione delle debuttanti, "highlight" della serata, ha costituito quest'anno uno spettacolo vero e proprio. Nove graziosissime ed eleganti ragazze, insieme ai loro partners, hanno eseguito una riuscitissima allegoria "Il tempo" ispirata alla "Danza delle ore" di Ponchielli. Il pubblico ha sottolineato con scroscianti applausi l'esecuzione dei vari quadri, che attraverso un sapiente gioco di luci hanno creato un'atmosfera suggestiva e aderente ai simbolismi espressi dai quadri stessi. Bravissimi organizzatrice e regista, la signora Attard presidente del Comitato femminile del Club Marconi.

MINERVA Studio
719 PUNCHBOWL ROAD PUNCHBOWL, N.S.W., 2196
PHONE: 759-3296

Il gruppo delle debuttanti e dei loro cavalieri. Al centro, la presidentessa del Comitato femminile del Club Marconi signora Attard, organizzatrice e regista della sfilata, della presentazione e del quadro allegorico "Il tempo".

L'ingresso e la sfilata delle debuttanti

Un particolare dell'esecuzione del quadro allegorico "Il tempo".

Women's Day Weekly 1973

SYDNEY
Saturday, June 30

WITH HAIR still in place from expert care, I was able to share several important functions with EG. First of all at Bankstown, where the council has built an Entertainment Centre. This has a huge auditorium, three small reception rooms (called appropriately Boronia, Acacia, etc), and a small theatre which seats 350.

Gordon Chater was among the special guests for the day and particularly appreciated the theatre.

We had a beautifully planned, well-cooked meal with the Mayor and Mayoress and other dignitaries before the grand opening by the PM — all in the Mayor's own entertainment section.

I've just one small query about lifts after mounting the super stairway. Stairs are okay when one is hale but not too good if one is aged or infirm. There is, however, a goods lift which can also carry passengers if necessary.

Was reminded of the lift routine in Moscow when I was there three years ago — two small cage lifts in a huge hotel were almost always there to take you up but *never* to take you down.

A similar situation comes about in city stores while the power strike is on. Escalators take us up but remain rigidly in place when we need to make the return journey. There's something quite awful about walking down a stationary escalator.

On Saturday night we received debs at the ball at the Marconi Club at Bossley Park. Old friends all, there, and the president and Mrs Zadro making us feel so welcome. It was our first visit since EG became PM and the garlanding of the ballroom and lavish entertainment made it a special night for all.

Came home laden with flowers — a basket of Australian wildflowers from Bankstown (particularly appropriate) and a huge bouquet of carnations and orchids and violets from the Marconi.

SYDNEY

1973 Editorial by Margaret Whitlam

"GRAN GALA" AL MARCONI CLUB

Il primo ministro al ballo delle debuttanti

SYDNEY, 4 luglio

COME abbiamo dato notizia nell'edizione di lunedì, la sera di sabato scorso nell'accogliente salone del Club Marconi ha avuto luogo il ballo delle debuttanti. La manifestazione ha ottenuto un successo senza precedenti. Il ballo è stato organizzato dalla signora Attard, presidente del comitato femminile del Marconi, la quale ha presentato le debuttanti al primo ministro, on. Whitlam, ospite d'eccezione della serata.

La manifestazione, alla quale ha partecipato un pubblico numeroso ed elegante (circa 600 persone) è stata aperta con gli inni nazionali. Subito dopo la presentazione e il primo giro di danza delle debuttanti, il segretario-manager del Marconi, Frabboni, ha invitato al microfono il presidente del sodalizio italiano di Bossley Park, cav. Felice Zadro, il quale, a nome del comitato e dei soci, ha dato il benvenuto al primo ministro, alla sua gentile consorte e agli ospiti d'onore.

L'on. Whitlam (che al Marconi è, si può dire, di casa) s'è detto felicissimo di trovarsi ancora una volta fra gli italiani ed ha brevemente ricordato ciò che il governo laborista ha già fatto per gli immigrati, soprattutto nel campo della previdenza sociale e dell'assistenza. Appropriate parole di circostanza sono state poi pronunciate dal dr. Piccirilli, dell'Ambasciata d'Italia.

Fra i numerosi ospiti sono stati notati, oltre al primo ministro e ai deputati Klugman e Ferguson, il membro del consiglio legislativo del N.S.W., cav. F. Calabro, i signori Waterman e Barris del dipartimento dell'immigrazione, il dr. Piccirilli e il vice console dr. Mott, il sindaco di Fairfield, Turtle, e i rappresentanti di vari club.

Nel corso della manifestazione, allietata dal complesso del maestro Enzo Giribaldi e da un applauditissimo spettacolo di varietà, è stata servita un'ottima cena.

Nella foto. In alto: il primo ministro durante la presentazione della debuttanti. In basso: la signora Attard e, da sinistra, Josephine Del Giudice, Patricia Caretta, Gianna Raffaelli, Martez Pisani-Rossi, Diana Rosetto, Laura Maghet, Doris Fresch, Lorraine Fontana, Barbara Vellar.

(Foto Minerva Studio)

1973 Publication unconfirmed

VM/AC

7847

Consolato Generale d'Italia
Sydney

i2 - DEC 1974

4- E/9

Egregio Cavaliere,

ho il pregio di rimetterLe in allegato il Diploma relativo all'Onorificenza di Cavaliere dell'Ordine "Al Merito della Repubblica Italiana".

Distinti saluti,

IL CONSOLE GENERALE
(G. ALTOMARE)

Cav. Felice Zadro,
Club Marconi,
Middle Road,
Bossley Park.

Il Comitato della Festa della Fratellanza

Da sinistra: N. Flego, Carlo Zaccariotto, Livio Benedetti, Felice Zadro, P. Beda Barcatta, Mario Mura, P. Alberico Jacovone, Antonio Brescia.
Mancano nella foto: Frank Labbozzetta; Giuseppe Calabro; Franco Labbozzetta

Date unknown

Il Messaggio del Presidente
President's Message

Cari soci,

siamo giunti al decimo anno di vita del "Marconi" e sono orgoglioso, con voi, di essere stato presente fin dagli inizi e partecipe in tutti questi anni allo sviluppo del nostro Circolo, che e' sorto dal nulla ed ha saputo affermarsi nelle comunita' Australiana ed Italiana.

Il contributo dato dal nostro Circolo nel campo sociale, ricreativo e soprattutto morale a favore particolarmente dei nostri connazionali e' evidente dalla stima che godiamo presso le autorita' italiane e del prestigio che abbiamo acquistato con le autorita' australiane, e di cio' ne possiamo essere fieri.

Questa rivista vi dara' un'idea di quello che e' stato fatto, ma non dimentichiamo che la strada e' ancora lunga e che soltanto con l'unione e la collaborazione reciproca che abbiamo sperimentato nel passato riusciremo a raggiungere le alte finalita' che ci proponiamo per il futuro.

Il felice cammino percorso sia di buon auspicio per il successo di domani.

FELICE ZADRO

Dear Members,

We have reached the 10th year of Club Marconi's life and I am proud to be able to say that I have partecipated to all these years of costant progress, from a humble beginning in 1958 to a respected and prosperous place in the community.

The contribution that our club has given in the social field, particularly amongst the italian nationals, is evident in the esteem in which the club is held by the Italian authorities and in the prestige we enjoy with the Australian authorities. Of this we can all be proud.

This review will give you an idea of what has been done, but let's not forget that the road ahead is still long and that only with the unity and mutual co-operation we have experienced in the past, we will succed in reaching the high aims we have set ourselves for the future.

Let's hope that the way so far travelled together with mutual understanding, be auspicious of the success of tomorrow.

FELICE ZADRO

1978 Club Marconi magazine

MEMBERS' HONORS LIST

O. MICHELINI
First President
Life Member

V. FIORELLI
Second President
Life Member

C. PANTANO
Third President
Life Member
Knight Italian Republic

F. ZADRO
Fourth President
Knight Italian Republic

E. DEL PIN
First Life Member
Knight Italian Republic

R. SARTOR
Life Member

P. SARTOR
Life Member

R.A. BAGATELLA
Life Member

L. GAUNA
Knight Italian Republic
Cavaliere del Lavoro

D. ZADRO
Knight of the
Italian Republic

P. DE MARTIN
Knight of the
Italian Republic

F. CALABRO
Alderman Fairfield Council
Former Mayor of Fairfield
Knight Italian Republic

O. CANTARELLA
Knight of the
Italian Republic

R. TERONE
Alderman of
Fairfield Council

K. MAKEPEACE
Alderman Fairfield Council
Former Mayor of Fairfield.

I. THORLEY
Alderman Fairfield Council
Former deputy - Mayor
of Fairfield

E.L. BEDFORD
Member of the Legislative
Assembly for Fairfield
Deputato al Parl. Statale

L. ZAMPROGNO
Life Member

1978

Couple's golden years

FELICE and Rina Zadro agree their years together have been "tempe di oro" or golden times.

The Bossley Park couple celebrated their 50th wedding anniversary last month with a mass at St Gertrudes Catholic Church at Smithfield and a dinner at Club Marconi with family and friends.

Felice – a founding member and former president of Marconi – says his wife is just as beautiful as the day they first met in 1936.

He came to see Rina's father about fixing his truck and caught sight of the young Rina scrubbing the kitchen floor. But Rina said she had an interest in him before then because of his "fair skin and black curly hair".

Felice said the marriage was successful because Rina is "very intelligent and well educated".

Rina says Felice was always a caring man and a good father even during tough economic times.

She has always supported her husband in his community activities. Felice is a former president of the Fairfield Multicultural Society. Felice and Rina both came to Australia from Italy before the 1930s. Felice worked as a vegetable gardener and then as a fruit growers' agent.

One of the highlights of his life was flying with aviation pioneer Charles Kingsford-Smith in Merriwa in 1934.

Felice and Rina were married at Fairfield's Our Lady of the Rosary Church on June 14, 1941.

Rina and Felice Zadro ... celebrating 50 years of marriage

1991 Publication Unconfirmed

Co. As. It. ITALIAN ASSOCIATION OF ASSISTANCE
(A COMPANY LIMITED BY GUARANTEE)   A.C.N. 002 288 539

4th Floor
2 Holden Street
Ashfield NSW 2131
Telephone: 798 7222
Facsimile: 716 6235

19th September, 1996

Cav. Felice Zadro
105 Bossley Road,
BOSSLEY PARK NSW 2176

Dear Mr.Zadro,

You have recently been nominated for a Co.As.It. Medal and it gives me great pleasure to inform you that your nomination has been successful.

The Medal will be presented at the Co.As.It. Dinner Dance to be held on Friday 18th October, 1996 at the Conca D'Oro "Classic Lounge" commencing at 7.00pm.

We hope that you will accept this Medal and join us as our guest (2 complimentary tickets) on this special occasion. It would also be greatly appreciated if you could keep your acceptance confidential at this stage.

If we can be of some help in organising a table on your behalf, do not hesitate to call Luisa Fontana at Co.As.It. on ph: 9798 7222. (tables seat 10 guests, tickets $35.00)

Once again congratulations and thank you so much for all you have done for Co.As.It.

Yours sincerely,

Cav. G. Fin OAM
President

il presidente Scalfaro si intrattiene a parlare con Felice Zadro, uno degli ex presidenti del Club Marconi.

il presidente Scalfaro si intrattiene con Angelo Bagatella, ex presidente del Club Marconi, e con il socio onorario a vita Tarcisio Sartoretto

il presidente Scalfaro riceve un omaggio dal presidente della Camera di Commercio Italiana di Sydney, Nick Scali

il presidente Scalfaro si congratula con Maurizio Pagnin, addetto alle relazioni pubbliche del Club Marconi e maestro di cerimonia durante l'incontro tra il primo cittadino italiano e la comunita` italiana al Club Marconi.

Salvatore (Sam) Bianca, operation manager del Club Marconi, nonchè bravo pittore, dona uno dei suoi quadri a Marianna Scalfaro. Assistono allo storico evento il presidente Scalfaro e il presidente Labbozzetta.

il presidente Scalfaro, alquanto allegro, si intrattiene con (da sinistra a destra) Tony Campolongo, Frank Carioti, Peter Grippaudo, Pat Sergi e il presidente del Club Marconi Tony Labbozzetta

PER RIVEDERE I LUOGHI DELL'INFANZIA

Tornano dall'Australia dopo quasi cinquant'anni

I fratelli Rina e Pietro Spinelli, che erano emigrati da Roncaglia con la famiglia, sono arrivati in questi giorni con i rispettivi coniugi - L'abbraccio con i parenti Vogliono conoscere l'Italia (ma «tifano» per la squadra di calcio australiana)

I fratelli Rina e Pietro Spinelli, al centro, con i rispettivi coniugi. (foto Cravedi)

(N.B.) - Dopo 47 anni due fratelli piacentini sono tornati dall'Australia per rivedere il luogo d'origine, Roncaglia, e per riabbracciare i parenti. I due fratelli sono i sigg. Rina e Pietro Spinelli, di 52 e 49 anni, che hanno approfittato di un giro turistico attraverso l'Europa per rivedere il paese da cui emigrarono giovanissimi. Dopo aver visitato l'Inghilterra, la Francia, la Spagna e il Portogallo, l'altra domenica sono giunti in Italia accompagnati dai rispettivi coniugi. La signora Rina ha sposato un emigrato italiano, il sig. Felice Zardo, originario di Pordenone, ex agente di compravendita di ca-

se ora in pensione. Hanno quattro figli (Arturo, Paolina, Giuseppe e Maria) tutti sposati che li hanno resi nonni di sette nipoti. Dal canto suo il sig. Pietro, ingegnere meccanico, ha sposato un'australiana, la sig.a Josè Denise, ed ha un figlio di 22 anni, Terry, laureando anch'egli in ingegneria meccanica. I fratelli Spinelli, che abitano vicino a Sydney, hanno visitato tutta la provincia e in particolare Roncaglia e Fossadello dove abitano le zie materne Albertina e Pia. Il vero festeggiamento per il loro ritorno si è avuto, però, domenica scorsa a Piacenza in casa della cugina Domenica Castal-

di Panni che abita sul Facsal con il papà Alessandro, di 82 anni. Parlando stentatamente l'italiano, quel tanto però necessario per farsi comprendere, i due fratelli hanno affermato che da tempo desideravano venire in Italia e che li ha commossi il fatto di aver incontrato a Roncaglia alcuni che ricordavano ancora il loro papà il quale, appassionato di musica, aveva allestito in paese la banda. Con cordialità mista a rimpianto sono stati ricordati lontani episodi che hanno fatto perno intorno ai loro genitori, Edoardo e Angiolina, che sono morti in Australia rispettivamente nel '41 e nel '70.

Benché fosse preso dall'importanza dell'avvenimento, il sig. Pietro, appassionato di sport, non ha trascurato di seguire i mondiali di calcio restando amareggiato, ma senza disperare per i prossimi incontri, per la prima sconfitta di quella che è ormai la sua squadra, l'Australia.

Dopo la sosta a Piacenza, i fratelli Spinelli con i rispettivi coniugi, hanno intrapreso un lungo viaggio attraverso l'Italia prima di tornare a casa. Vogliono conoscerla direttamente dopo averne sentito parlare a lungo dai genitori quando bambini chiedevano notizie della terra in cui erano nati.

Date unknown

Spark that kindled fame

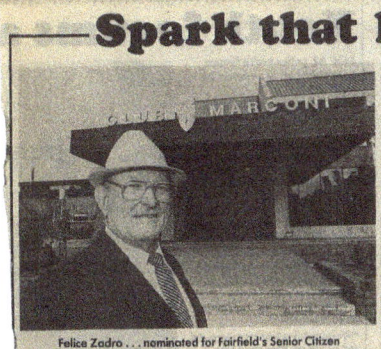

Felice Zadro ... nominated for Fairfield's Senior Citizen Award

ONE night on a farm near Merriwa, Felice Zadro became part of an Australian legend.

After migrating from Italy with his family in 1929, Mr Zadro worked at a Merriwa sheep station, saving money to buy land for a market garden at Smithfield.

One evening, his boss told him to set fire to six bales of hay in a paddock. The burning bales served as crude landing lights for Australian aviation pioneer Charles Kingsford-Smith. Kingsford-Smith touched down at Merriwa as part of a tour to raise money for his famous flight from England to Australia in 1934.

"I had the privilege to fly with Kingsford-Smith — I'm very proud to have been part of that piece of Australian history," Mr Zadro said.

After working at Merriwa for about five years, Mr Zadro bought land at Smithfield with his father. They worked the farm into a successful market garden and in 1941, Mr Zadro married Rina Spinelli.

Mr Zadro has continued to play a significant role in Australian history, helping other Italian migrants settle in Fairfield and founding what is perhaps the Italian community's most famous institution — Club Marconi.

In recognition of all his work, Club Marconi has nominated him for the Fairfield City Chamber of Commerce and Industry Senior Citizen of the Year Award.

He has donated incalculable hours for various organisations including the Smithfield Soccer Club and St Gertrudes Catholic in Smithfeild.

He began the English and Italian classes which continue to provide an important service to club members.

In 1967 he was made a Knight of the Italian Republic by the then President Giuseppe Sarragut.

"I attribute my achievements to the support I've had from everybody," he said. "I would like to be remembered best as a good Italian because only a good Italian can be a good Australian."

2000 Fairfield Advance

Lunedì 24 gennaio 2000 — **Cronache di Sydney** — **LA FIAMMA 41**

Nominato dal Fairfield City Council in occasione dell'Australia Day

Felice Zadro cittadino dell'anno

Connazionale distintosi per intelligente altruismo e fattiva collaborazione

SYDNEY - E' un connazionale l'Australia Day Citizen of the Year del 2000 della municipalità di Fairfield e si tratta di Felice Zadro, che dal suo arrivo in Australia nel 1929 ha svolto un eccellente continuo lavoro a favore della nostra comunità. Ex presidente e co-fondatore del Club Marconi, Felice Zadro, 86 anni, di Bossley Park, è un personaggio molto conosciuto nella nostra comunità: padre di 4 figli con 13 nipoti e 4 pronipoti.

Nel rendere nota la nomina il sindaco della Città di Fairfield, Anwar Khoshaba, ha sottolineato che Zadro è un perfetto esempio di quello che rappresenta la Città di Fairfield con la sua diversità culturale che si inserisce nella comunità australiana. Il sindaco ha continuato ricordando che Felice Zadro è venuto in Australia per cercare migliori condizioni di vita e nel suo cammino ha saputo offrire un aiuto alla sua comunità in diversi modi. Dopo essersi stabilito nella zona di Fairfield-Smithfield, all'inizio degli Anni '30, ha iniziato la sua attività di assistenza agli immigrati italiani svolgendo lavoro di interprete ed aiutandoli a trovare un lavoro e ad acquistare la casa. Durante la seconda guerra mondiale è stato vicepresidente della NSW Vegetable Growers Association e portavoce della stessa associazione per la zona metropolitana. Zadro è sempre stato un forte sostenitore dello CVO e dello Smithfield Soccer Club e si è generosamente adoperato per la raccolta di fondi a favore della chiesa cattolica S. Gertrude di Smithfield, della scuola cattolica e del coro parrocchiale. Socio fondatore del Club Marconi ha attivamente lavorato per la formazione del Marconi Youth Centre.

In qualità di presidente del Club Marconi ha collaborato attivamente con il Co.As.It. nell'assistenza degli immigrati italiani che giungevano in Australia senza alcuna conoscenza dell'inglese e di riconoscimento del suo lavoro nel 1967 è stato nominato cavaliere all'ordine del merito della Repubblica Italiana.

Successivamente è stato eletto presidente della Multicultural Society Fountain Committee ed ha collaborato alla costruzione di una fontana pubblica a Fairfield e alla formazione di un comitato che ha raccolto $20,000 per la chiesa e la scuola di Bossley Park.

L'awards verrà consegnato a Felice Zadro dal sindaco di Fairfield,

Felice Zadro, ex presidente del Club Marconi, personaggio di rilievo della comunità italiana

Anwar Khoshaba, al Fairfield Council Chambers, Avoca Rd, Wakeley, mercoledì 26 gennaio alle 19.30.

La comunità italiana è altamente onorata di questo meritato riconoscimento di un connazionale che ha saputo distinguersi in Australia per intelligente altruismo e per la sua fattiva collaborazione a tutte le proposte di incoraggiare gli altri nei loro ideali e di antiarli nelle loro necessità.

La sua dedizione ad iniziative di notevole importanza ha contemporaneamente fatto conoscere in questo paese la parte più nobile dell'animo degli italiani, esercitando un trascinante esempio per chi lo circondava e portando alto il nome dell'Italia. Di questo non solo chi ha largamente beneficiato della sua volontaria attività di Felice Zadro ma anche noi tutti suoi connazionali gli siamo profondamente grati.

Sussidi governativi alle organizzazioni sportive consegnati dal ministro Sandra Nori

SYDNEY - L'on. Sandra Nori, deputato statale per Port Jackson e ministro del Turismo e dello Small Business, ha consegnato mercoledì 19 gennaio i contributi del governo ai rappresentanti delle organizzazioni sportive e ricreative del suo elettorato.

Nel corso della cerimonia della consegna degli assegni il ministro Nori ha sottolineato che i fondi governativi assegnati a questo settore hanno il compito di sviluppare le attrezzature sportive e ricreative e renderle accessibili a tutti i cittadini.

Per il settore sport e ricreazione al seggio elettorale di Port Jackson sono stati assegnati $48,175, ora suddivisi alle varie organizzazioni: al Leichhardt Wanderers Junior Rugby Football Club $15,000 per l'istallazione dell'impianto di illuminazione del Blackmore Park; alla North Western Suburbs Tennis Association $10,000 per la sistemazione delle tribune e delle tettoie al Birchgrove Park; al Leichhardt Municipal Council $12,500 per attrezzature di ginnastica al King George Park; Alla Annandale Public School $10,000 per la sistemazione del cortile della scuola; $675 sono

Il ministro Sandra Nori con i rappresentanti delle associazioni sportive ai quali ha consegnato i sussidi

stati assegnati al King George Oval per l'istallazione di due porte.

Il supporto per lo sviluppo di queste attrezzature fa parte dell'impegno del governo di incoraggiare uno stile di vita sano per tutte le sezioni della comunità.

Martedì 25 gennaio sul Canale 7 il concerto dell'Australia Day

SYDNEY - Martedì 25 gennaio si terrà il concerto denominato "Qantas Spirit of Australia Day" con la partecipazione di un coro di 520 giovani australiani che tributeranno un corposnovo omaggio alla nostra nazione cantando "I Still Call Australia Home".

Il programma include anche l'esibizione di numerose star quali: The Seekers, Christine Anu, Iva Davies, Troy Cassar-Daly, James Blundell, Adam Brand e Sharon Millechip, Vanessa Amorosi, Tenor Australian e Todd McKenney.

Il concerto prevede l'esecuzione di molte canzoni classiche australiane come: "Way Out West", "Great Southern Land", "Waltzing Matilda", ecc.

"Advance Australia Fair" e "I Am Australia".

Il Qantas Spirit of Australia Day Concert sarà presentato da Stan Grant e Anne Fulwood e trasmesso su tutta la rete nazionale dal Canale 7 a partire dalle 19 di martedì 25 gennaio.

La memoranda serata di divertimento culminerà con l'annuncio futturo dal primo ministro, on. John Howard degli Australian Achiever Awards e dell'Australian of the Year Award.

Nel frattempo è già stata annunciata la nomina dello Young Australian of the Year nella persona di Ian Thorpe, il diciottenne di Sydney che ha già conseguito grandi successi nel nuoto.

2000

Our quiet achiever

by MARNIE O'NEILL

THE people of Fairfield have a lot to thank Felice Zadro for - without him there might not have been a Club Marconi.

But co-founding the Italian flagship was just one of his many achievements that moved Fairfield Council to name Mr Zadro the city's Citizen of the Year.

"I am somewhat bewildered but very, very flattered," the modest 86-year-old told the *Advance*.

"When we established Club Marconi 27 years ago we were really just looking for a place where we could drink beer legally.

"One day we were all sitting around outside drinking beer and the police came and they confiscated the beer so we said 'Why don't we build a club where we can sell beer legally and watch sport'."

The rest is history.

Mr Zadro was also behind the Marconi Youth Centre – the first youth service in south-west Sydney. Soon after, the managers of Blacktown Workers Club were

AUSTRALIA DAY HONOUR ROLL
Citizen of the Year: Felice Zadro
Young Citizen of the Year: Michael Garrett-Meade
Cultural Medallion: Savannairand Kay
Achievement Award: Butch Chapman
Achievement Certificates: Buu Tran, Kellie Linow, Jocelyn Giles, Dorothy French, Irene Mao

calling Mr Zadro for advice on how to build their own.

But Mr Zadro was making waves long before then. From the moment he sailed into Sydney from Italy to be reunited with his father in 1929 he gave everything he had to offer.

After settling in the Smithfield area in the early 30s Mr Zadro assisted other new migrants to the area by playing interpreter, finding them work and helping them buy land on which to build their homes.

He went on to aid groups like the Smithfield Catholic Youth Organisation and Smithfield Soccer Club by donating transport and goods and raised funds for St Gertrude's Catholic Church in Smithfield, the nearby Catholic school and parish choir.

During World War 2 Mr Zadro was vice-president of the NSW Vegetable Growers Association and acted as its metropolitan spokesman.

But asked which is his proudest achievement Mr Zadro picks none of the above.

"My greatest achievement was bringing four Australians into this world," he said, referring to his two daughters and two sons.

Mr Zadro and wife of 59 years Rina also have 13 grandchildren and four great-grandchildren.

Fairfield mayor Anwer Khoshaba called Mr Zadro "a fine example of what Fairfield represents with its cultural diversity combining with Australian mateship".

"Mr Zadro came to this country seeking a better life for himself which he achieved and along the way has helped his community in quite a number of ways," he said.

Citizen of the Year Felice Zadro ... 'I am somewhat bewildered but very, very flattered'.
PHOTO: Matthew Vasilescu

FAIRFIELD CITY Champion

Wednesday, January 26, 2000 — A FAIRFAX COMMUNITY NEWSPAPER — Ph: 9725 6755 — Classifieds: 13 24 25

WINNERS!

Cowboy's dream

FELICE Zadro has been named Fairfield City Council's Australia Day Citizen of the Year.

Mr Zadro, 86, is well-known to the community as a former president and co-founder of Club Marconi.

The Bossley Park great-grandfather has presided over the birth and growth of one of Australia's largest multicultural communities based at Fairfield.

It was a simple photograph of his father on horseback in the Australian outback which drew Mr Zadro halfway around the world from his birthplace in Italy about 70 years ago.

"I pictured myself as a cowboy on horseback," Mr Zadro said.

He arrived in Australia in 1929 at age 16, and over the years worked as a jack-of-all-trades including station hand, a farmer, in real estate, and selling vegetables at Sydney markets for many years.

When he settled in Smithfield with his wife Rina to raise a family, he found there was a need to help migrants in the Fairfield-Smithfield area by acting as interpreter.

He helped them to find employment and to purchase their first home in Australia.

He also sponsored many families.

Mr Zadro has assisted local groups like the Smithfield Catholic Youth Organisation and was instrumental in raising funds for the construction of St Gertrude's Catholic Church in Smithfield and the Catholic School nearby.

He formed the local parish choir which was conducted by his brother David.

Mr Zadro was an original founder of Club Marconi, and instigated the formation of the Marconi Youth Centre.

He was on the board of directors for 27 years and president of the club from 1966 to 69, and 1971 to 73.

"These were the hard years financially for the club but we managed to overcome all our difficulties and continue with our progress, Mr Zadro said.

"The first members contributed fifty pounds each and we drew our membership numbers out of a hat. I drew out membership number eight. I still have this number and I am also a life member."

Mr Zadro became president of the Multicultural Society, originally formed by then Fairfield Mayor Keith Makepeace to build a monument to recognise the contribution of the various nationalities in the Fairfield area.

■ FELICE Zadro is pictured on page one, bottom left.

FAIRFIELD City Council's Australia Day Award Recipients are: **Australia Day Citizen of the Year:** Felice Zadro. **Australia Day Young Citizen of the Year:** Michael Garrett-Meade (see page five). **Australia Day Cultural Medallion:** Sovannairand Kay. **Australia Day Achievement Medallion:** Butch Chapman. **Australia Day Achievement Certificates:** Buu Tran, Kellie Linow, Jocelyn Giles, Dorothy French and Irene Mao.

CLUB MARCONI Celebrating 45 years

From a humble start

FROM little things, big things grow.

Club Marconi can trace its origins to a shed in rural Bossley Park in the 1950s, set up as a meeting place for Italians.

It is now one of the most famous landmarks in the region – and its membership is as multicultural as Fairfield itself.

Club chief executive officer Debbie Foening said the club since 1958 has helped shape the city's lifestyle.

"I'm sure each and every one of you have some wonderful memories that have been made at our club and we invite you to celebrate with us throughout August," she said.

"We also pay tribute to the members of our community and club who have made our existence possible, those being the foundation members."

A host of activities are planned, detailed in this 18-page feature.

The *Champion* joins the community in wishing Club Marconi a happy birthday and a prosperous future.

Police beer raid launched an icon

By LAURA SPERANZA

FELICE Zadro is a proud man. As a founding member of Club Marconi, he looks back on its 45-year history with fond memories.

After all, the place he helped to build and develop in the 1960s is still growing in a new century.

"Club Marconi is like the fruit in my garden; it is always blooming," he said with a smile.

Mr Zadro, 90, said the idea to build a club happened over a game of bocce with his mates, a group of local Italian settlers.

"We were playing at the bocce courts in Horsley Park and we got a little thirsty so we brought along some beer," he said.

"The police confiscated the beer because we didn't have a licence.

"So we thought, why don't we build a place where we can meet socially.

"It was an amazing time for us as we saw our dream come to life.

"Club Marconi was built by passionate volunteers, both Italians and Australians, who contributed time and money.

"Club Marconi stands as a proud reminder of the work of Italian settlers in Australia."

Mr Zadro started its youth centre which organised activities and outings for members' children, was involved in establishing soccer as a sport at the club and was club president 1966-69 and 1971-73.

Mr Zadro said the club has become

How a game of bocce started it

part of his family which includes his wife of 61 years, Rina, their four children, 13 grandchildren and 11 great-grandchildren.

Granddaughter Loretta McPherson couldn't agree more.

"Ever since I was a child, we came to Club Marconi for the chestnut festival and other events," she said.

"The club was a lot smaller in those days but there was still a lot of activity happening.

"I took tennis lessons there and also went to Italian language class, and then later on I had my 21st birthday there and went to the Sunday night disco in the 1980s.

"Club Marconi is part of my memories as much as my grandfather's."

Now she comes to watch the soccer with her husband, coach Eddie McPherson of the Club's under-17s side, and their sons Benjamin, Thomas and Matthew.

"The Club has changed physically, but the atmosphere is still the same," she said.

"There is something always familiar and welcoming about it – it's great to run into people you know every time you visit."

GENERATIONS OF MARCONI . . . Felice Zadro with grand-daughter Loretta McPherson who said: "Club Marconi is part of my memories as much as my grandfather's." Photo: KRISTY HUNTER

FAIRFIELD ADVANCE, Wednesday, October 15, 2003

NEWS

CELEBRATING 45 YEARS: Club Marconi presidents, past and present, Tony Campologno, Frank Fontana, Felice Zadro, Angelo Bagatella and Tony Labbozzetta.

Marconi milestone

MEGAN PARIS

AT 90 years of age, Felice Zadro's association with Club Marconi is as deeply embedded as the foundations of the Bossley Park club themselves.

As a foundation member and former president, he joined three other former presidents and the current president at lunch to celebrate the 45th anniversary of the club's formation.

Mr Zadro's passion for the club spans 45 years of memories and experiences, of how he first became involved in the club and how the idea to build the club came over a game of bocce with his friends, a group of Italians who had settled in the area.

"The police confiscated the beer because we didn't have a licence. So from that we thought, 'why don't we build a place where we can meet socially?'."

In the early stages of the club, Mr Zadro involved himself in the creation of the youth centre, which was built at the same time as the club's main hall.

He was so enthusiastic about the youth centre that the president, Vic Fiorelli, said to him "it is yours to look after".

Mr Zadro then created a committee to be responsible for the many functions, concerts and events that were to be held at the new venue.

He also introduced groups such as the Marconi Choir and Italian classes.

Angelo Bagatella was one of very few people at the club who could speak and write English. This knowledge helped the integration of Italians with the Australian community, using sports as the key.

"In one day we had 27 different sporting groups competing at Marconi," Mr Bagatella said.

Passionate about soccer, longest-standing president Tony Labbozzetta's initial association with the club was the successful promotion of its soccer team from second to first division.

He played a key role in amalgamating the soccer association with the social club and under his presidency members saw the introduction of a childcare centre, a junior disco, sporting facilities and events.

When Frank Fontana joined the club in 1958, he travelled daily from North Sydney to meet his friends.

"I was at the first meeting when we decided to call our venue Club Marconi," said Mr Fontana, who has played an integral role in the introduction and development of sports such as netball and cycling.

Current president Tony Campologno was named Italian of the year for 2003 from the National Migrant Association of Australia and America.

Mr Campolongo, a former mayor of Fairfield, now oversees one of the most powerful clubs in the country, with a membership of about 25,000 made up of 120 different nationalities and more than 400 staff members.

2005

Society seeks listing

Fairfield International Monument.

PHILIP HENDERSON

FORMER members of the defunct Fairfield Multicultural Society will continue their push for the Fairfield International Monument to be heritage-listed.

Fairfield Council recently assumed responsibility for the landmark, which has stood in Fairfield for more than 50 years, after the society handed over the last of its remaining monument funds to Mayor Nick Lalich.

But the society's last president Roland Melosi confirmed former members would still be involved in the monument's future.

"We're looking at trying to get it heritage-listed down the track," Mr Melosi said of the landmark, currently situated along The Crescent in Fairfield's town centre.

"We're working on it right now."

Felice Zadro, a founding member of the society, and one of the original group which championed the monument in the 1960s, said the society wanted to ensure the

OBJECT OF PRIDE: Felice Zadro and Roland Melosi have called for the heritage listing of the Fairfield International Monument. Photo: NICK ANDREAN

historic landmark remained for future generations.

"I feel very proud that the council has taken responsibility for the monument because of what it represents to the community," he said.

"It should be an object of pride for Fairfield as recognition for all the people and cultural groups in the city. We hope generations will continue to honour the monument throughout the years."

Driven by then Mayor Keith Makepeace, the society was formed in 1962 by 16 people from different cultural backgrounds to honour the many nationalities settling in the area.

The monument was originally installed as a fountain along The Horsley Drive but was moved to its current location in the late 1980s.

Cr Lalich said the the landmark represented the co-operation which formed the backbone of Fairfield's tolerant and vibrant city.

"The International monument will be a feature in any redesign work we do in The Crescent Park and the money will be used to improve the monument's appearance," he said.

Govt fails on drug promise

PROSPECT Federal Labor MP Chris Bowen says the Federal Government has not delivered on its Pharmaceutical Benefits Scheme election promise.

During the federal election the Government announced savings would be made through the application of a 12.5 per cent reduction to the cost of generic pharmaceuticals.

However, Mr Bowen said the 12.5 per cent cut to a particular group of similar drugs would occur only once – when a new generic drug of that group was introduced.

He said this decision protected brand-name manufacturers and made it more expensive for families in Prospect to treat illness.

Funds boost for roads

THE federal electorates of Prospect and Fowler will receive $100,000 and $200,000 respectively in Federal Government funding for "black spot" road safety improvements.

Single-lane roundabouts will be installed at the intersections of Fairview Rd and Longfield St in Cabramatta, and the intersections of John St and Lord St, and St Johns Rd and Harrington St, in Cabramatta West.

The money for Prospect will go to construction of a single-lane roundabout at the intersection of The Boulevarde and Evans St in Fairfield Heights, and a raised pedestrian crossing and refuge at the intersection of Hamilton Rd and Lackey St in Fairfield.

2005 / 2006

NEWS — Wednesday August 11 2004

PLAQUE... From left: Multicultural Society president Roland Melosi, founding member Wally Friend, Janice Crosio, Mayor Nick Lalich, founding member Felice Zadrow and Tony Campolongo.

Multicultural plaque unveiled

A plaque to members of the Fairfield Multicultural Society was unveiled at Fairfield's International Monument on Saturday.

The plaque tells the story of the monument and honours the people that formed the society.

Fairfield Mayor Nick Lalich said that the monument was a well-known landmark in Fairfield and that the plaque provided information that added significance to Fairfield's heritage.

"In 1968, the Fairfield National Society was formed by migrants from 16 nations who were committed to a harmonious and coherent society, proud to be Australian yet enthusiastic to share and embrace cultural difference," Cr Lalich said.

"Since then, the Fairfield Multicultural Society, as they are now known, has made a big contribution to our community."

The society helps worthwhile causes through fundraising.

It has helped organise and promote many functions, festivals and concerts.

The monument was dedicated to Fairfield by the society to acknowledge and promote community harmony and migrants' contribution to Fairfield.

YOUR SAY *Wednesday August 18 2004*

Funding for our railways

LET YOUR VOICE BE HEARD: Send your letters to Your Say, c/o *Fairfield Champion*, PO Box 905, Fairfield, NSW 1860. Email: jmcgill@mail.fairfax.com.au Fax: 9727 6281. Include your name and address for verification. Letters may be cut for space, clarity or legal reasons. Letters may be republished on the internet or by other methods. The views expressed are not necessarily those of the editor or staff.

Critical problems are facing the travelling public on NSW rail services.

It is disgusting how the railway bureaucrats and our state politicians have let the railways deteriorate as if a bomb has hit.

It is caused by the push by the transport lobbies and politicians to have the railway freight/passenger services privatised.

Just look at the millions of taxpayers' dollars being spent by the previous transport minister, Carl Scully, on roads and tunnels etc. Why doesn't Transport Minister Michael Costa get the same amount of money to spend on the railway to bring the railways to where they were in the late 1960s and early 1970s – one of the world's best and safest.

We need a hands-on railway commissioner and an assistant to take full control of NSW railways with a vision to modernise stations and trains and do away with unproductive areas such as public spokesmen.

The Maldon-Dombarton-Port Kembla rail line must be completed to take freight trains to the South Coast instead of freight going from the Sydney end.

TERENCE APPS
Lansvale

Unity celebration suffers an insult

Thank you for the news item (*Champion*, August 11) about the unveiling of the multicultural plaque and the large section allocated to the readers' letters.

Some 30 years ago when a pound was worth a pound, encouraged by the mayor of Fairfield (the late Keith MacPeace), existing ethnic communities at that time raised £30,000 to build a memorial for the future generations. To the joy of us all, a beautiful fountain was erected in the eastern part of Fairfield. It would have been standing there today, enjoyed by locals and visitors.

Unfortunately, the fountain had to be moved to a more visible position because of a few two-legged "animals" who began damaging the structure.

The structure was moved to Railway Park. A beautiful spot. Fairfield Council went out of the way to set up nice tables and benches around the International Monument.

Another group of "animals" took the place over. Wrecked the lovely tables and benches. Enjoy, you mugs, now sitting on a cold grass. Hope you will get piles one day. Saturday, August 7, was a beautiful day. The International Monument and the area never looked better, thanks to the Mayor, Nick Lalich, and his administration who again went out of their way to install a plaque with a brief history of the International Monument.

Its unveiling was attended by living foundation members, local identities Felice Zadro, Wally Friend and Janice Crosio of the old Fairfield National Society. Following the ceremony and a cup of coffee, the Mayor and Mrs Crosio enjoyed the hospitality with our leaders in the community.

Three days later, August 11, I nearly had a heart attack. Some "animals" must be still alive. The plaque is damaged. A name attempted to be erased. What do you do with these animals?

Somebody knows who did it. If you are a citizen of Australia then go to the police and admit it. If not, then go to some inaccessible place and break your leg.

[NAME AND ADDRESS SUPPLIED]

16 FAIRFIELD ADVANCE, Wednesday, November 28, 2007   www.fairfieldadvance.com.au

Art to honour Fairfield legends

The Zadro family – Arthur Zadro, son of Felice Zadro, his wife Caroline, mother Rina (seated), granddaughter of Felice Zadro Loretta McPherson and Mayor Nick Lalich unveil the artwork created in the multiculturalism advocate's honour.
Picture: NICK ANDREAN

SEAN PLAMBECK

THREE men from separate eras and walks of life were honoured on Friday for their shared dedication to adding to Fairfield's distinct character.

Colonial medical pioneer Dr William Bland, Olympic swimmer Michael Wenden and multiculturalism advocate Felice Zadro each had a monument to their accomplishments unveiled on Ware St.

The late Mr Zadro helped develop the city's market gardens, its sense of cultural cohesion and Club Marconi.

His wife Rina and son Arthur were among those who gathered in the CBD to see the public art work for the first time.

"He was a very modest man and he only did what in his heart he felt he had to do," Mrs Zadro said.

"He loved people and this community and I believe his upbringing had a lot to do with how he lived because he was a man of great faith."

Fairfield Mayor Nick Lalich had the task of revealing the monuments. He said all of those honoured had helped to make Fairfield a better place.

"They are important Australians who have contributed to our nation in many different ways and we are very proud of their close link with Fairfield," he said.

DR WILLIAM BLAND
Dr William Bland was born in England. In 1813, while serving in the navy, he killed a man in a dual of honour and was sentenced to seven years transportation.

Arriving in Sydney in 1814 he was sent to work as a doctor at the Castle Hill Lunatic Asylum. Pardoned after serving a year of his sentence, he then set up the first private medical practice in the colony. He was jailed for a year in 1818 for making fun of Governor Lachlan Macquarie.

He was one of the instigators of the push to representative government, and in 1843 was elected to the first Legislative Assembly.

FELICE ZADRO
Felice Zadro was a pioneer of Italian settlement in Fairfield. He migrated from Italy in 1929.

Mr Zadro played a significant role helping other Italian migrants settle and was a founding member of Club Marconi, and was also behind the Marconi Youth Centre.

He also donated incalculable hours of volunteer service to various organisations.

MICHAEL WENDEN
Michael Wenden was an Australian freestyle swimming champion and attended Patrician Brothers Fairfield.

During his career, which spanned the years between 1966 and 1974, he competed in 100m and 200m events at the 1966, 1970 and 1974 Commonwealth Games, and the 1968 and 1972 Olympics.

2007

Fairfield City Champion, Wednesday, December 12, 2007 -21

Proud: Rina Zadro (sitting) was at the unveiling of new art work dedicated to her late husband, Felice. She was joined by her family (also pictured) and Fairfield Mayor Nick Lalich (far right). Mr Zadro donated countless hours of his time to local groups such as the Smithfield Soccer Club, the Smithfield Catholic Youth Organisation, and St Gertrudes' Catholic Church and school in Smithfield. **Picture: Elliott Housego**

Local heroes honoured

THREE respected Australians with close links to Fairfield have been honoured with artworks in Fairfield town centre.

Last month, Mayor Nick Lalich unveiled artworks honouring Felice Zadro, Michael Wenden and Dr William Bland – three men who have made significant contributions to Australia.

"The Faces of Fairfield art work celebrates the substantial contributions of past and present Australians, and their links with Fairfield," Mr Lalich said.

Felice Zadro was a pioneer of Italian settlement in the Fairfield area.

One of the founding members of Club Marconi, he was also behind the Marconi Youth Centre – the first youth service in south-west Sydney.

As a former convict and Australia's first private doctor, William Bland was elected to the first NSW Legislative Assembly in 1843.

His country estate, Mark Lodge, covered the present day business area of Fairfield.

Despite storm damage, a 13 metre, evergreen oak tree planted by Dr Bland in 1850 still stands in Oakdene Park and is listed as a state heritage item.

Champion swimmer Michael Wenden went to Patrician Brother in Fairfield. Wenden won the 100 metres and 200m freestyle gold medals at the 1968 Olympic Games in Mexico City, and also competed in Munich four years later.

He went to three Commonwealth Games between 1966 and 1974 and won nine gold medals, including three in the 100m freestyle.

2008 Fairfield Advance — Italian Republic Day Festa
Advertising Feature

Club Marconi's foundation board of directors (above) in 1958. Below: the main entrance to the club in 1958.

From bocce club to cultural centre

FROM modest beginnings, Club Marconi has grown into a thriving cultural centre, Sydney's truly cosmopolitan club.

The idea of opening an Italian club became a reality on July 21, 1958, when a humble bocce club opened with 108 members.

From just 2ha of farmland, the club has grown into a social and cultural icon, a fully-licensed registered club that sits on more than 12ha of parkland and playing fields, boasting more than 26,000 members and 350 staff.

Contrary to its origins of serving the Italian public, Club Marconi now provides sporting, entertainment, educational and social facilities for the entire community.

It's membership base represents 18 nationalities and more than 24 languages.

The first Italian Republic Day Festa was celebrated in 2005, as a result of club president Tony Campolongo's desire for Western Sydney residents to celebrate Italy's national day.

Mr Campolongo said it was particularly vital the event was held for the senior members of the Italian community, many of whom maintained a strong bond with their homeland.

The event now attracts visitors from all many parts of Sydney, with 30,000 expected this year.

Members to share an historic moment

THIS year's Italian Republic Day celebrations mark a historic moment for Club Marconi and its local community.

Sydney's "truly cosmopolitan club" is turning 50 in August and is ready to celebrate in style with every member receiving a ticket to one of the anniversary dinners being held that month in the club's auditorium.

Members also have the chance to win fabulous travel prizes in the $35,000 Mystery Flight and Caribbean Cruise 50th Birthday Bonanza.

Club Marconi will be giving away 12 mystery flights to destinations in Australia and the South Pacific every Monday, Tuesday and Wednesday night in August.

On Sunday, August 31, members will have the chance to win an MSC Caribbean cruise with flights including a luxurious three-day stop-over in Miami - valued at more than $12,000.

Anniversary dinner guests will be treated to a scrumptious meal accompanied by live entertainment, a special DVD presentation and a trip down memory lane with a visit to the Marconi Museum.

The museum brings the rich history of the club alive, with its myriad historical memorabilia and items of interest dating back to 1958.

Guests will be able to see artefacts relating to membership, club boards, uniforms, football, special events as well as administration documents.

Club Marconi will also release a limited edition commemorative book, containing an in-depth recap of the club, including an array of memorable images and interviews with community members who have been a part of its growth and advancement.

Holiday delights there for taking

PINING for a holiday? Head to the festa this weekend when Club Marconi will give away $6000 in travel packages and flights, courtesy of Travelscene Horsley Park.

Destinations to be won include a trip to picturesque New Zealand and a romantic Hamilton Island getaway.

To go into the draw for the packages, visit the team on Republic Day at the Travelscene Horsley Park and MSC Cruises tents and fill out an entry form.

The winner will be announced at 7pm.

Be present at the main lounge to find out if you will be packing your suitcase.

ACKNOWLEDGEMENTS

At time of publication, it's been twenty-five years since I sat down with Nonno in the formal living room in Bossley Park, and yet when I read through these pages, it brings his voice back to my mind in a heartbeat. He had a thick Italian accent; I never even noticed it until I listened back to the tape recordings. It was just him.

Nonno also had a few funny turns of phrase, such as: *'Don't trip over the apple-pie cart'*, and he used to say, quite a lot, *'Like nobody's business'*, to mean something indescribable. For example, when talking about his mother, he would say, 'My mum was amazing. She looked after us like nobody's business.' He would say it with a slight outbreath that summoned an immenseness to the feeling, coupled with a quick wistful look to the horizon, in which he re-lived a fleeting happy memory, whilst love shone in his eyes, that only grief can muster.

I've carried the cassette tapes that these many conversations were recorded on through multiple house moves, and over more than two decades of life, coupled with the transcriptions that were done initially on a transcribing machine with a foot pedal to stop and rewind the tapes. I was twenty-one when I started out on this journey, and Nonno's voice has accompanied me through all my travels, work, love, life, and motherhood.

If I sat down with him now, my questions would have been informed by the grooves of age. I would have pressed him more on his regrets, the challenges of running a business, keeping love alive, the pressure of being a breadwinner, governance issues, politics, climate change, technology, and probably even AI, just to seek his wisdom. He would have had something to say about it all, some nugget of hard-won insight earnt in a completely different context, relevant for the moment. However, even though I didn't get to ask him all I needed to navigate adulthood, his words have provided me with an immense depth of perspective and wisdom that I have and will continue to draw down on, for a long time to come. It has been an extraordinary gift to have had these words in my heart and mind for all this time.

To the Italian community of Western Sydney, thank you for the striving, hard work, anguish, graft, faith, toil, generosity, hope, the longing, and most of all the love.

You came together when you needed it most to navigate a strange and foreign new world. You've built an extraordinary legacy of community and cultural pride, and a safe place to call home for thousands, if not millions of people. Your impact lives on, it cannot be measured or contained.

I would like to sincerely thank my editors, my word-whiz mum, Caroline Zadro nee Agius, who has always been my first editor, for everything; her grammar-radar as sharp as her guidance. Thank you to my father, Arthur Zadro, who helped me fact check. The book has been a great conversation starter for the sharing of his stories, and I'm grateful that my dad entrusts me to his story as well.

To Georgia Took, who polished again, and helped me bring together the photos, and to David Jenkins, who helped me frame the author's note and the tone of my personal contributions.

Thank you to Joseph, Pauline, Maria, and my dad, Arthur, for being supportive of me putting this book together. I hope you hear your dad's voice and feel like I do, that I've just visited, had a fresh pot of hot tea, a biscuit or two, and had some great conversations with them both.

To my cousins, who share our Nanna and Nonno; Adrian, Loretta, Jerome, Mark, Peter, Catherine, Natalie, Angela, Karinna, Simon, and my siblings, Adam and Elizabeth, and to your partners, and children—gosh, we were lucky to be loved, and cherished, and challenged, and taught, and cared for, and feed, and nurtured … *like nobody's business*— in a million ways by them both. I know you miss Nanna and Nonno, as much as I do.

I hope Nanna and Nonno's twenty-six great-grandchildren we brought into the world get to know Nonno a little through these pages. I hope it helps you to show them, where you came from.

I love how we all grew up together, a tribe celebrating everything from New Year's Day to all the birthdays, Easter, Christmas, Father's Day, Mother's Day, the graduations, the births, the baptisms… they were the best of times. I'm grateful to you all. And especially to our parents who made this all happen for us and kept us close. It is a very special gift. A lifelong treasure of love and memories.

And finally, to my Georgina, who inspired me to finish this journey, I love you more than all the stars in the universe.

Felicity Zadro, 2024.

ABOUT THE AUTHOR

Felicity Zadro, 2024.

Felicity Zadro was born in Western Sydney, Australia. She holds degrees in social sciences and communications from UTS Sydney. In 2007 Felicity founded a brand and communications agency and named it after her grandfather. She lives in Leichhardt, NSW Australia with her daughter Georgina.

www.ingramcontent.com/pod-product-compliance
Lightning Source LLC
Chambersburg PA
CBHW061216070526
44584CB00029B/3852